The COVID-19 Crisis

Key Social and Psychological Issues

Eric D. Miller
Kent State University

Series in Sociology

VERNON PRESS

In the Americas:
Vernon Press
1000 N West Street, Suite 1200,
Wilmington, Delaware 19801
United States

In the rest of the world:
Vernon Press
C/Sancti Espiritu 17,
Malaga, 29006
Spain

Series in Sociology

Library of Congress Control Number: 2022950347

ISBN: 978-1-64889-876-1

Also available: 978-1-64889-587-6 [Hardback]; 978-1-64889-691-0 [PDF, E-Book]

Product and company names mentioned in this work are the trademarks of their respective owners. While every care has been taken in preparing this work, neither the authors nor Vernon Art and Science Inc. may be held responsible for any loss or damage caused or alleged to be caused directly or indirectly by the information contained in it.

Every effort has been made to trace all copyright holders, but if any have been inadvertently overlooked the publisher will be pleased to include any necessary credits in any subsequent reprint or edition.

Cover design by Vernon Press using photography by Elizabeth McDaniel on Unsplash.

This book is dedicated to my mother with much love and gratitude

Table of Contents

Foreword   vii
John Harvey
University of Iowa

Preface   ix

CHAPTER ONE
**The Covid-19 Pandemic: How Did This Happen and
Psychology's Role**   1

CHAPTER TWO
Key Political Dynamics of COVID-19   13

CHAPTER THREE
Economic Fears and Threats   27

CHAPTER FOUR
Personal and Interpersonal Challenges   39

CHAPTER FIVE
Loss, Grief, and Mental Health Concerns   51

CHAPTER SIX
Challenges to Select Populations   59

CHAPTER SEVEN
The Psychology of Good and Evil in the Covid-19 Pandemic   73

CHAPTER EIGHT
The Psychology of Place and Environment Post Covid-19   87

CHAPTER NINE
Online and Virtual (Learning) Worlds   99

CHAPTER TEN
Epilogue: Where Do We Go From Here?   109

Index   121

Foreword

John Harvey

University of Iowa

Eric Miller has a history of being one of the most insightful and timely researchers and theorists about topics relevant to loss and trauma. As a 27-year member of the editorial board for the *Journal of Loss and Trauma*, he has helped shape the field of loss and trauma and has been a leader in developing ideas and theories pertaining to significant loss events such as the Pittsburgh Synagogue Shooting. In this same vein, in the present book, he has addressed the Covid-19 Pandemic with new ideas and a broad moral understanding of how this great loss event has affected and will affect generations of people world-wide.

The present book is one of the first on this topic. It is written in such a way that scholars, practitioners, and the general public will find it to be highly readable and insightful. Millions of people have died as a direct or indirect effect of the Covid virus. Scholars such as Miller help us understand how individuals, families, communities, and countries have attempted to deal with the Covid crisis. This pandemic will likely not be the last. Hopefully, it will not be the "new normal," in reference to the term mentioned in Miller's introduction. This pandemic deserves the type of analysis and scholarship so richly displayed in this book. Miller's voice must be heard and appreciated if we are to successfully deal with the long-term impact of this deadly disease.

John Harvey, Professor Emeritus, University of Iowa, Founding Editor of *Journal of Loss and Trauma*.

Preface

One of the leading scientific voices during the Covid pandemic, Anthony Fauci, delivered his first public address on the virus in late January 2020, titled "Coronavirus Infections: More Than Just the Common Cold" (American Society for Microbiology, 2020). Most anyone who lived through the Covid pandemic would very likely say that was an understatement—though perhaps, as discussed in this book, a better way to have phrased this point may have been that most everyone *should* have come to that conclusion (and, alas, may have held views anathema to such renderings).

When I first considered this book project, it was after the completion of a journal article written in March/April 2020 in which I termed the then-early-stage pandemic as "the loss and trauma of our time" (Miller, 2020). I will leave it to others to entertain whether that description was appropriate or even prescient. This book largely picks up where my 2020 journal article left off. But, at the time of this writing in February 2022, I would still suggest that this phraseology was indeed appropriate. Why so? In brief, as considered in this book, the pandemic itself produced many direct effects on individuals and society-at-large that have been (at the very least) challenging if not traumatic and even disturbing. As I also explore in this book, the pandemic has arguably been connected to other secondary effects and consequences--some of which may ultimately prove to be beneficial to many individuals, while others may have quite disruptive or nefarious impacts. As an example of the latter, this preface was written days after the Russian invasion of Ukraine--which is largely viewed as the most significant war event in Europe since World War II (e.g., Hirsch, 2022). At first blush, while it might seem questionable to link that event with the pandemic, a major theme considered in this book is that the pandemic has produced much instability and has showcased American vulnerabilities (in particular). (And, a secondary and unknown question is whether this warlike incursion will have any impacts on the development of the virus itself (Park, 2022).) But of course, as I caution in this book, it is difficult to try to pinpoint clear cause-and-effect conclusions linked with the pandemic. However, in reflecting on terming the pandemic as the "loss and trauma of our time," the potential circumstances of any sort of nuclear exchange as a result of this conflict—however unlikely, though plausible (Giovannini, 2022)—makes this aforesaid description almost pale by comparison.

It is my hope that readers will agree that I have mindfully attempted to document a critically important ongoing historical event from a psychological perspective. This point helps to make this book a fairly unique and major contribution that distinguishes it from other works regarding the Covid pandemic. As such, this book might also serve as a sort of historical document that future scholars, teachers, and students of history may want to refer to as a source when considering psychological responses to this crisis from its earliest phases. In discussing some of the major psychosocial effects and consequences of the pandemic, readers will also find that this book draws from a large variety of both media and academic sources; in doing so, it aims to be accessible to a more general public while still maintaining appeal and interest to scholars and teachers alike—which is a fairly daunting task in and of itself. This book has timely social relevance of a continuously evolving and socially stigmatized experience in its focus on highlighting the chief developments (predominantly) from the first two years of the Covid pandemic with a psychological lens. In sum, academics, clinicians, policy makers, students, and laypersons who seek to have a critical yet concise overview of some of the most compelling psychological issues related to the pandemic from its earliest stages should find this work a helpful reference.

As previously noted and as I discuss in the first chapter, this brief book is meant to provide a sampling of many key issues and themes largely emanating from the first two years of the pandemic that should have much relevance to psychological and social scientific perspectives. Most of this analysis is particularly (though not necessarily exclusively) focused on events and happenings as they developed in America for two basic reasons: (1) the pandemic has had particularly insidious effects on America and (2) trying to bridge the knowledge and understanding of some of the more unique realities and contours regarding the pandemic response from different countries requires a more sensitive and extensive approach beyond the scope of this book. At the time of this initial writing in late February 2022 and following the Omicron surge, it was unclear if the health threats associated with the pandemic have truly subsided—or whether, (as has often been shown during the pandemic) most individuals are just desperately clamouring to return to "normalcy" while refusing to appreciate the continued possible future health risks and threats (Browne, 2022). It is indeed possible that, as we learn more about the pandemic's (direct and indirect) effects over time, readers may have somewhat different interpretations of these events depending on whether this book is being reviewed years—or decades—following its release. Even so, it is my fervent hope that this fairly concise book offers scholars, students, and laypersons alike a sense of these initial issues and topics as they arose from the first two years of the pandemic.

As a reader, at this point, you may be wondering a bit about my background as I begin to discuss some of the key social and psychological issues emanating from the Covid pandemic. It is true that my perspective is just that. All of us who have lived through the pandemic will likely hold their own personal views about its effects for both ourselves and society. Certainly, I do not claim to possess an all-knowing insight about the pandemic's psychological effects, nor would I claim any absolute resolution about its future trajectories. Nevertheless, this book was written with my informed scholarly and research background and training in the field of personality and social psychology. As a scholar who has published several books and academic papers largely focused on how adults adjust to loss and adverse events, I might add that I have many broad interests across and beyond the field of psychology that also helps to inform my scholarly perspective. Given the far-reaching scope of the Covid pandemic, this approach should also be welcomed and displayed throughout much of this book as well.

When I reflect on some of the effects that the pandemic has had on my life, I am reminded of the brief essay by communications scholar Peter Joseph Gloviczki who shared some of his initial reactions to the start of the pandemic in the same published journal volume as my aforementioned paper (Gloviczki, 2020). Among his comments were as follows:

> Today is March 18, 2020. I woke up this morning to an actual fog outside. Fitting, amidst the COVID-19 virus, how it is pressing us to reconsider what we know to be clear…With the daily development of the virus, I wonder where we will be in one week. I had been looking forward to traveling today. Postponed for now, in the way the best place for anyone to be amidst our transnational moment is inside…I continue my daily routines. Treadmill, pushups, texting. I stay mostly indoors. I take reasonable steps to try and follow the guidance. I wait for my work to reopen, to reunite with students so that we might continue our lessons. Is COVID 19 our new normal? I hope not. I am longing for clarity, for what was normal: a familiar way of going forward (Gloviczki, 2020, p. 558).

To me, in many respects, Gloviczki's comments take me back to my own initial shock that we were facing a global pandemic (coupled with dubious political leadership and guidance)—and the angst over what the future may bring. Like Gloviczki, I recall the early days—and weeks—of remaining solely indoors (including to do exercise) until there was a bit more guidance and understanding of what we were potentially dealing with in regard to the virus. As his comments also hinted, most of us found a way to go on living after this initial shock subsided. That is a testament to the resiliency showcased by many during times of crisis. While much of this book highlights this theme, this analysis does not shy away from some of the darker behaviors depicted during early phases of the pandemic.

There are many individuals I would like to thank and express acknowledgment for in regard to the preparation of this book. Let me first thank the excellent guidance and support offered by Vernon Press, with particular appreciation to Victoria Echegaray and Argiris Legatos for their initial interest in my proposal as well as to Julien Verdeaux for much guidance throughout the review process. I am also very thankful for the reviewers of this book who have offered much helpful and thoughtful input that, in turn, has strengthened its contents and organization. On a personal note, as expressed in my dedication, I am forever grateful to all of the love and support provided to me by my mother, Ruth. The pandemic, in particular, brought many challenges—big and small—and she indeed is a great model of resilience herself. I thank my entire family as well with a particular acknowledgment of the many challenges that the pandemic created for my two sons—and their great ability and resilience to stay true to the phrase made popular by the British government in the early phases of World War II to "Keep Calm and Carry On." I would be remiss if I did not also acknowledge my beloved dog, Pepper, as our regular long walks were of tremendous personal value to me in coping with the many challenges during the pandemic.

References

American Society for Microbiology. (2020, January 30). Anthony Fauci addresses coronavirus. *American Society for Microbiology.* https://asm.org/Articles/2020/January/Anthony-Fauci-Addresses-Coronavirus

Browne, E. (2022, January 16). Lifting mask mandates too soon puts U. S. at risk of future COVID variants. *Newsweek.* https://www.newsweek.com/too-soon-us-states-drop-face-mask-mandates-future-variants-1679854

Giovannini, F. (2022, February 27). A hurting stalemate? The risks of nuclear weapon use in the Ukraine crisis. *Bulletin of the Atomic Scientists.* https://thebulletin.org/2022/02/a-hurting-stalemate-the-risks-of-nuclear-weapon-use-in-the-ukraine-crisis/

Gloviczki, P. J. (2020). Longing for a familiar way of going forward. *Journal of Loss and Trauma, 25*(6-7), 558-559. https://doi.org/10.1080/15325024.2020.1746072

Hirsch, M. (2022, February 24). Why Putin's war is the West's biggest test since World War II. *Foreign Policy.* https://foreignpolicy.com/2022/02/24/russia-ukraine-war-west-world-war-2/

Miller, E. D. (2020). The COVID-19 pandemic: The loss and trauma event of our time. *Journal of Loss and Trauma, 25*(6-7), 560-572. https://doi.org/10.1080/15325024.2020.1759217

Park, A. (2022, March 2). Why Ukraine's COVID-19 problem is everyone's problem. *Time.* https://time.com/6153254/ukraine-russia-war-covid-19/

CHAPTER ONE

The Covid-19 Pandemic: How Did This Happen and Psychology's Role

Why I Termed the Covid-19 Pandemic as the "Loss and Trauma of Our Time"

Between the time period of mid-March to mid-April 2020, I authored a paper in the *Journal of Loss and Trauma* where I termed the Covid-19 pandemic as the "loss and trauma event of our time" (Miller, 2020). The decision to use this bold language was quite purposeful as the potential for this pandemic to have far-reaching effects on society seemed apparent. While I hardly would claim any clairvoyant abilities, my reasoned scientific analysis helped me reach this possibility and was largely built around three guiding ideas: (1.) an appreciation of the seriousness of the virus itself; (2.) a concern regarding (particularly the American) political and governmental responses to the crisis; and (3.) a concern over how willing or able the public-at-large would be to proceed with necessary health measures to curtail the adverse effects of the pandemic.

There were a few notable areas that this paper did not clearly predict from the earliest days of the pandemic to about two years hence. Though this paper did warn of political strife and upheaval, the absolute backlash against select health practices, such as mask-wearing, was not fully initially realized. When I was writing this article, the notion that a safe and effective vaccine might be developed by the end of 2020 probably would have seemed like a dreamlike fantasy to many. But, of course, with the initial release of the Pfizer vaccine (and subsequent others such as Moderna), the hope that perhaps the pandemic might somehow come to an "end" became a real prospect. Indeed, all previous pandemics have proven that they do, in fact, end. However, my initial analysis failed to consider a large segment of society would opt to not be vaccinated. To quantify this point further, in late September 2022, a few weeks after the CDC approved the latest Covid (bivalent) booster (designed to target the common BA.4 and BA.5 Omicron subvariants), around 80% of the U.S. population had at least one shot as of that date and 68% had the requisite two shots to be fully vaccinated per CDC guidelines; however, at this particular time, there was growing concern from health professionals that relatively few eligible Americans (i.e., less than 4%) had received this booster (Bendix, 2022). Indeed, my paper failed to fully explore or appreciate the potential for variants of the virus: The fact that the Delta (and later) Omicron variants proved to be significantly more transmissible than the original virus, coupled with the large number of unvaccinated individuals, left this potential "end" of the pandemic much more murky—even as President Joe Biden (somewhat dubiously) declared that "the pandemic is over" around this time in September of 2022 (Bendix, 2022).

This brief book expands on many of the themes contained in my original 2020 paper and resumes the story of the Covid pandemic from when I first wrote about it in March and April 2020. This book should not necessarily be viewed as a complete and thorough examination of a timeline of how the first two years of the pandemic unfolded per se—that is, from around the time the virus was first noted in Wuhan, China in late December 2019 through the end of 2021. Rather, this book largely examines many of the key select events and critical developments during this time period with an emphasis on important psychological and social science-related issues. Though the pandemic has, of course, impacted the world, this book is predominantly focused on how it impacted American life; a chief reason for this decision is due to the fact that (as of December 2021) the United States led the world in cases and deaths attributed to Covid as well as a widespread belief that leadership on the pandemic (particularly in its earliest months) had been exceedingly poor (The New England Journal of Medicine Editors, 2020).

COVID-19 as a Macabre Experiment

Anyone who has ever had a basic introductory course in general psychology (or related fields, particularly in the social sciences) is likely very familiar with the saying that "correlation does not imply causation." This basic truism has been demonstrated with many colorful examples, such as consumption of a favorite treat, ice cream, and its ostensibly harmful associations such as with an increased risk of shark attacks (Siegel, 2019). Even though ice cream consumption tends to increase as the incidence of shark attacks does as well, it would be absurd to presume that either variable was the clear causal effect or consequence of the other. What would best explain this association is the fact that both events are most apt to occur in the summer. That is, ice cream consumption tends to increase during warmer periods as do (the relatively rare) occurrences of shark attacks when individuals are most likely to swim in the warmer ocean.

To clarify, this is not to say that exploring associations between variables is a meaningless endeavor. For instance, among a bevy of related studies, Jacob et al. (2018) found that smoking tobacco was associated with the increased risk of developing one of 25 different cancers. This basic behavioral pattern has been repeatedly shown as being (among other reasons) a key rationale for why most physicians warn against the health consequences and hazards of smoking. The point of this example is to suggest that even though we must be quite cautious and wary of drawing causal associations between correlated variables, this is not to suggest that such relationships are somehow meaningless.

As the aforementioned example clearly suggests, social scientists have long appreciated the value that such quantitative methods have for nonexperimental research as well as qualitative methods that include grounded theory and ethnographic and narrative perspectives including methods (i.e., mixed methods) that utilize both approaches (e.g., Edmonds & Kennedy, 2017). Regarding the latter point, many scholars (like Ellis, 2018) have documented how qualitative work can often ascertain what motivates individual behaviors in a deeper and personal fashion. Even so, one with a basic understanding of research methodology would appreciate that there is a way to more clearly discern cause and effect—that is, with the use of experimental methodologies. Such methods, in their most basic sense, would involve the manipulation of at least one (independent) variable by the researcher in order to observe its effect of at least one other (dependent) variable, which is an important goal of scientific research given its ability to provide explanations of behavior. This design is not without its shortcomings, insomuch that experimental designs are often criticized for their inability to clearly relate to real-world phenomena.

This aforesaid concern is largely irrelevant to studying the psychological effects of the pandemic insomuch that understanding its impact on individuals certainly represents an extremely important real-world event. In fact, one scientific, journalistic report referred to select gender differences regarding how women were more likely than men to adhere to social lockdowns as representing a sort of "live social experiment" (Study Finds, 2021). Another report suggested that the pandemic represented "a huge natural experiment" though added some caution about drawing clear casual conclusions (Rosen, 2021). This latter point is particularly important to appreciate since no study that attempts to understand the various impacts that the pandemic has had on individuals and society can ever truly pinpoint cause and effect. There are also clear limitations on the types of variables that researchers can ethically manipulate. As an example, while we can study how unemployment impacts individuals and their families, of course, researchers would not be able to necessarily assign individuals to different conditions—including those that would result in job loss. Though this crisis represents a sort of naturally occurring quasi-random control trial (Humphreys, 2020), without such random assignment and manipulation of independent variables, causality will necessarily be at least dubious.

Even if understanding the effects of the Covid-19 pandemic (which will, from this point forward, predominantly just be referred to as Covid) cannot truly represent the clear causality found with "true" experiments, it does represent a sort of macabre natural experiment. Researchers routinely study how events impact people and society. Prior to the pandemic, arguably one of the best contemporary examples of this involved an examination of the effects of the September 11, 2001 terrorist attacks. The specific research methodologies that were noted earlier are among the various ways and means that researchers studied 9/11 and will likely continue to understand the impact of the Covid pandemic on individuals and society. Harrison (2021) offers a summary of the various lines of research from just *one university*—New York University, which is located in the general area of the World Trade Center—that emanated over 20 years since the 9/11 attacks. She summarized some of the areas of research as follows: the psychological impact of the attacks (for various populations), health effects particularly to those who were exposed to dangerous materials (related to the attacks), preparing for future threats, Lower Manhattan's socioeconomic recovery, law, policy, architecture, and culture post-9/11, and ways of utilizing creative expression as a means of healing from the attacks. This non-exhaustive, interdisciplinary list of research knowledge from just one university regarding 9/11 offers a sense that the Covid pandemic will likewise be replete with a wide array of scholarly inquiry and pursuits over the coming decades.

Just as we could, in theory, try to examine changes pre- and post-9/11, researchers and other scholars are actively attempting to do this with respect to the pandemic. But, once more, such research is a reminder that a naturally occurring event—like 9/11 or the Covid pandemic—cannot necessarily provide clear evidence for cause and effect. This book also considers other extremely significant events—like the murder of George Floyd and the January 6, 2021 U.S. Capitol attacks—that occurred during the pandemic. While one might consider how the pandemic may have contributed to these events (as this book does), we cannot conclusively say the pandemic caused them. Frankly, these two events—or another very critical event that occurred nearly two years into the pandemic, the 2022 Russian invasion of Ukraine—could also be analyzed through such a pre- and post-event perspective as well. For instance, regarding the latter event, though scholars and health professionals alike realized that this invasion would have a devastating impact on the well-being of the Ukrainian citizenry in particular (Patel & Erickson, 2022), it was also suggested that it would need to be understood not just through the influence of the pandemic (Moiseenko et al., 2022) but even with the additional (though unlikely) threat of a nuclear exchange (Bollfrass, & Herzog, 2022).

Thematic Analysis of Dimensions of COVID-19: New York City in the Aftermath of Crisis and Political Divisions over Mask Wearing in Online Contexts

With a realization that those reading this book may potentially be doing so many years in the future, this section details thematic analyses of two different critical issues surrounding the Covid pandemic that I conducted in the summer of 2020. To those readers, in particular, it seemed fitting to try to provide some context for how the Covid pandemic was initially perceived as a disaster and why mask-wearing was often such a contentious issue given its clear importance to mitigating the virus' effects on public health. To that end, the first analysis featured a comparison of two different YouTube videos of the "street level" aftermath approximately one-week after two different crises in New York City: the 9/11 terrorist attacks and the height of the first Covid surge. The second analysis considered why some individuals may have chosen to not wear a face mask as depicted in the written comments from a liberal-leaning and conservative-leaning online news periodical. As hypothesized, there were more varied emotions present and greater social interaction from the 9/11 video than the Covid video. As expected, the more conservative article featured more comments highlighting personal freedoms as reasons to not wear face masks, whereas the more liberal-leaning article largely expressed disbelief or disgust over those who chose to not wear one.

To offer a bit more detail, through thematic analysis, this investigation addressed two critical issues emanating from the earliest phases of crisis: understanding its unique dimensions as a disaster and possible political motivations for face mask wearing. Indeed, it can be ethically challenging to assess human responses to disaster soon after a crisis. Yet, the Covid crisis may have unique qualities that differentiate it from other disasters including the 9/11 terrorist attacks (e.g., Saltzman et al., 2020). This investigation offered a rather unique way of trying to describe depicted images from New York City presented in two different YouTube videos very soon after the 9/11 attacks and the peak of the April 2020 Covid death rate in New York City. In doing so, it highlighted some of the expected unique qualities that the Covid crisis posed (such as social isolation) that distinguish it from other disasters.

Despite the highly effective practice of wearing face masks in mitigating the spread of Covid, there is evidence that conservatives were less likely to support taking such precautions (Corpuz et al., 2020). The second part of this investigation considered possible reasons as to how individuals who may be more predisposed to a conservative versus liberal political ideology approached the seemingly controversial issue of wearing face masks in America by reviewing online comments from a more liberal and conservative leaning online newspaper article.

These two thematic analyses utilized Braun and Clarke's (2006) methods of becoming familiar with the data, generating initial codes, and searching for and naming themes. Upon doing a cursory examination of these materials, I anticipated the following general themes. Regarding the YouTube videos, I anticipated there being more varied emotions present and greater social interaction from the 9/11 than the Covid video, which may suggest greater social distance and less varied emotion. Regarding the two newspaper articles, I expected more comments featuring themes of highlighting personal freedoms as reasons to not wear masks in the conservative article and expressed disbelief or disgust over those who choose not to wear a face mask in the liberal one.

This thematic analysis was granted an Institutional Review Board (IRB) Level I approval since all materials involved publicly available archival data where all personally identifiable information was removed. The utilized online materials are described below fairly generically to further ensure confidentiality and privacy (though the data sources utilized for this study are available from the corresponding author on reasonable request).

The first video showed about 9 minutes of footage from September 17, 2001, predominantly focused on public streets blocks away from the site where the former Twin Towers were destroyed and had around 17,000 views. It captured "everyday life" from that particular moment in time where individuals were walking around the area and other related images. The second video, which had around 212,000 views at the time of this investigation, showed a YouTube vlogger walking from Times Square to Union Square and captured images of New York City streets and sights along the way for about 52 minutes on April 16, 2020, which, quite notably, was about a week or so following the height of the curve of deaths in New York City from the first Covid wave.

The first news article was from a July 1, 2020 (liberal leaning) *HuffPost* paper titled "The Psychology Behind Why Some People Refuse To Wear Face Masks" and, at the time of the investigation, had about 140 comments. The second article was from a July 21, 2020 (conservative leaning) *Breitbart* (often referred to as *Breitbart News*) article titled "Donald Trump: Wear a Mask, They Have an Impact" and had approximately 6,000 comments.

As previously noted, the methods of Braun and Clarke (2006) were utilized for all of these materials. By definition, this thematic analysis did not have set codes for any of these materials. For the YouTube videos, any noticeable theme present was noted. For the comments from the online news articles, the most prominent themes derived from examining the comments as to why individuals might choose to not wear face masks were noted.

Table 1 lists the key theme categories and how they were presented in the 9/11 and Covid videos, which involved the following: the presence of wearing face masks, presence of crowds and their emotional displays, key activities shown and the activity level, store status, police and military presence, salient focus of the tragedy, and the particularly unique feature from each video. As expected, there were more varied emotional reactions and greater social interaction in the 9/11 video. However, there were several unexpected findings such as the presence of wearing face masks in both videos and clearer sustained police and military presence and patriotic themes in the 9/11 video.

Table 1: Key Themes Present in the 9/11 versus COVID-19 Videos

Theme	9/11 Video	COVID-19 Video
Presence of Mask Wearing?	Yes	Yes
Displayed Emotion of Passersby	Varied (no overt distress; smiling/laughing shown)	Muted/stoic
Key Activities Shown	Talking to others (including cellphone); Walking; Eating; Smoking; Taking pictures of area	Walking; Biking
General Activity Level	Very crowded; Everyday activity	Little noise; Long stretches of no people
Stores	Largely open	Largely closed
Police/Military Presence	Both present and talking amongst each other and the public	Sporadic police cars
Salient Focus of The Tragedy	Extended Shots of World Trade Center ruins; Missing persons posters	Billboards and signage encouraging mask wearing, good hygiene, and thanking essential workers
Particularly Unique Feature on Each Video	Playing of patriotic music	Socially distanced long lines waiting to enter supermarket; Selling cleaning supplies outside

The following key themes were present from the comments contained in the two online articles denoting perceptions of face mask wearing. As expected, comments from the liberal-leaning *HuffPost* article, largely suggested that those who did not wear face masks either supported Trump, were acting vain, selfish, or lacking empathy, or simply uneducated or in denial about the science of the virus; very few comments considered a sense of distrust in the government or media. By contrast, the conservative-leaning *Breitbart* article largely featured comments suggesting that wearing a face mask was tantamount to being forced or controlled by the government and taking away personal rights. Three additional themes were also noted: masks do not work or are not effective, the virus isn't much of a threat, or such promotion was a ploy of liberal or Democratic policies.

Naturally, there are several limitations to this study insomuch that it features a more basic thematic analysis of select online materials. This thematic analysis also lacked the methodological rigor that would be expected in a more formal, systematic comparison of social media materials (e.g., Miller, 2015) and may underscore additional shortcomings of the investigation (such as the differing lengths of the videos and their selection criteria as well as the use of only two newspaper articles with an unbalanced sample size of comments). Even so, there were some definite advantages of utilizing these online publicly available sources. The YouTube videos uniquely captured the aftermath of these two different traumatic events in ways that standard psychological instruments could not and the comments from these articles likely reflected respondents true attitudes without as much concern for social desirability (as might be present in a more formal lab condition). Further, these two thematic analyses helped to provide some additional understanding of two critical issues present in the early phases of the Covid crisis.

The General Organization of This Book

This book has not been designed to explore or discuss every historical development as it progressed from the first two years of the pandemic—from the discovery of a mysterious outbreak in Wuhan, China in late December 2019 through the rise of another highly contagious variant—Omicron—that swept the world at the end of the year in 2021. In fact, given its particularly pronounced effects in American culture, much of this book will be especially focused on these effects. This book will also not detail or showcase a comprehensive review of all pertinent psychological or social scientific literature that has been published in the first two years of the pandemic. The previous section notwithstanding, readers of this book will not necessarily find new revelations about the pandemic per se—but perhaps may develop new insights about it.

After summarizing what this book is *not*, let me briefly highlight what readers may find intriguing and notable about this book. As previously noted, this book is an extension of my previous paper (Miller, 2020) which introduced the potential psychological fallout and effects of the pandemic. I have previously discussed (Miller, 2014) the academic value and merits of Ernest Boyer's (1990) somewhat hazy concept of the scholarship of integration—where bits and pieces of information are assembled and analyzed in a more novel way so as to provide new insights about a given issue. In that spirit, given the far-reaching effects that the pandemic has had on both individuals and society-at-large, this book was written to be approachable for academics, students, and laypersons alike. To further amplify this point, readers will find that an eclectic mix of both (largely online-based) news articles and analyses along with select academic papers and concepts are featured in this concise book. The inclusion of select news reports from the first two years of the pandemic helps to document how the pandemic was publicly presented—which, given the relatively ephemeral nature of the Internet, it can be especially helpful to document such sources.

The general chapter layout of the book henceforth is as follows. The next two following chapters focus on various political and economic consequences of Covid. In particular, Chapter two will explore how many politicians and political interpretations have guided and influenced the pandemic—quite often to the detriment of the public at large whereas Chapter three covers some of the key economic fears and threats associated with the pandemic. The next set of chapters consider some of the more personal and interpersonal challenges—along with mental health concerns and grief—in Chapters four and five, respectively. Chapter six offers an overview of some critical issues associated with select societal populations. Chapter seven explores the gamut of human behavior—from good to evil (with more of the focus on the latter)— during the first two years of the pandemic. Chapter eight offers some consideration of how the pandemic may have altered the places we have (or have not) gone to during this period. Chapter nine considers a different modality of place: That is, it addresses some of the dynamics of online and virtual learning contexts impacted due to the pandemic. Chapter ten concludes with some discussion of how we may live and continue to adjust to the pandemic and its effects in the years to come.

In my initial analysis of the pandemic (Miller, 2020), I noted how unfortunate it was that many historical events—such as with respect to the Holocaust and World War II—did not necessarily have clear documentation from psychologists as they had happened. Part of this was likely due to the fact that psychology—as an academic discipline and science—is still (historically speaking) a relatively newer field of inquiry that did not feature the methods and perspectives widely employed today. Of course too, we take for granted that we now live in a world where there is information regularly and easily shared with others—and clearly not the case when many historical events happened. For instance, it took well over a decade after the assassination of President John F. Kennedy before the infamous Zapruder film was widely shown to the larger public (English, 2012). Thus, it is hoped that both contemporary—and future—students may draw some new perspectives and insights from this book that will further guide their study of the initial psychological and social issues that dominated the pandemic.

References

Bendix, A. (2022, September 23). Less than 4% of eligible people have gotten updated Covid booster shots, one month into the rollout. *NBC News.*

https://www.nbcnews.com/health/health-news/updated-covid-booster-shots-doses-administered-cdc-rcna48960

Bollfrass, A. K., & Herzog, S. (2022). The war in Ukraine and global nuclear order. *Survival, 64*(4), 7-32. https://doi.org/10.1080/00396338.2022.2103255

Boyer, E. L. (1990). *Scholarship reconsidered: Priorities of the professoriate.* Princeton University Press.

Braun, V., & Clarke, V. (2006). Using thematic analysis in psychology. *Qualitative Research in Psychology, 3*(2), 77-101. https://doi.org/10.1191/1478088706qp063oa

Corpuz, R., D'Alessandro, S., Adeyemo, J., Jankowski, N., & Kandalaft, K. (2020). Life history orientation predicts COVID-19 precautions and projected behaviors. *Frontiers in Psychology, 11,* 1-9. https://doi.org/10.3389/fpsyg.2020.01857

Edmonds, W. A., & Kennedy, T. D. (2017). *An applied guide to research design: Quantitative, qualitative, and mixed methods* (2nd ed.). Sage.

Ellis, C. (2018). *Final negotiations: A story of love, loss, and chronic illness* (2nd ed.). Temple University Press.

English, J. (2012, March 6). On this date in 1975, Geraldo aired the Zapruder Film for the first time. *Mental Floss.* https://www.mentalfloss.com/article/30153/date-1975-geraldo-aired-zapruder-film-first-time

Harrison, J. (2021, September 1). Knowledge from tragedy: NYU research post-9/11. *NYU.* https://www.nyu.edu/about/news-publications/news/2021/august/nyu-research-post-9-11.html

Humphreys, A. (2020, August 8). 'Paranoid about the pandemic': How COVID-19 brought the 'largest criminology experiment in history.' *National Post.* https://nationalpost.com/news/paranoid-about-the-pandemic-how-covid-19-brought-the-largest-criminology-experiment-in-history/wcm/964870a2-86c8-4814-a34f-edf1bc76417e/

Jacob, L., Freyn, M., Kalder, M., Dinas, K., & Kostev, K. (2018). Impact of tobacco smoking on the risk of developing 25 different cancers in the UK: A retrospective study of 422,010 patients followed for up to 30 years. *Oncotarget, 9*(25), 17420-17429. https://doi.org/ 10.18632/oncotarget.24724

Miller, E. D. (2014). The academic psychologist as a convener of information: Implications for the scholarship of integration and (online) teaching. *New Ideas in Psychology, 33,* 35–45. https://doi.org/10.1016/j.newideapsych.2014.01.001

Miller, E. D. (2015). Content analysis of select YouTube postings: Comparisons of reactions to the Sandy Hook and Aurora Shootings and Hurricane Sandy. *Cyberpsychology, Behavior, and Social Networking, 18*(11), 635-640. https://doi.org/10.1089/cyber.2015.0045

Miller, E. D. (2020). The COVID-19 pandemic: The loss and trauma event of our time. *Journal of Loss and Trauma, 25*(6-7), 560-572. https://doi.org/10.1080/15325024.2020.1759217

Moiseenko, I., Shakhovska, N., Dronyuk, I., & Datsko, O. (2022). Social and economics aspects of the pandemic influence in Ukraine. *Procedia Computer Science, 198,* 670-675. https://doi.org/10.1016/j.procs.2021.12.304

The New England Journal of Medicine Editors. (2020). Dying in a leadership vacuum. *The New England Journal of Medicine, 383,* 1479-1480. https://doi.org/10.1056/NEJMe2029812

Patel, S., & Erickson, T. (2022). The new humanitarian crisis in Ukraine: Coping with the public health impact of hybrid warfare, mass migration, and mental health trauma. *Disaster Medicine and Public Health Preparedness*, 1-2. https://doi.org/10.1017/dmp.2022.70

Rosen, J. (2021). Pandemic upheaval offers a huge natural experiment. *Nature*, *596*(7870), 149-151. https://doi.org/10.1038/d41586-021-02092-7

Saltzman, L. Y., Hansel, T. C., & Bordnick, P. S. (2020). Loneliness, isolation, and social support factors in post-COVID-19 mental health. *Psychological Trauma: Theory, Research, Practice, and Policy*, *12*(S1), S55-S57. https://doi.org/10.1037/tra0000703

Siegel, E. (2019, January 19). Why ice cream is linked to shark attacks – correlation/causation smackdown. *Kdnuggets*. https://www.kdnuggets.com/2019/01/dr-data-ice-cream-linked-shark-attacks.html

Study Finds. (2021, September 29). COVID lockdown was a 'live social experiment' revealing how women, men behave during pandemics. *Study Finds*. https://www.studyfinds.org/covid-lockdown-social-experiment/

Chapter Two

Key Political Dynamics of COVID-19

This chapter gives consideration to select significant political and governmental agency failures during the first two years of the Covid pandemic. While a handful of successes are also identified, this analysis is particularly focused on the many strategic blunders that occurred during this period—and indeed, most of these responses were just that. Given that a much more sensitive and extensive approach would be necessary to make more concrete comparisons to the pandemic response between countries, this analysis is chiefly focused on the American response with select cross-cultural comparisons noted sparingly and only when particularly relevant.

A Global and Geopolitical Crisis

To say that we should never have dreamed of a punishing pandemic happening in the modern era would be a complete fallacy. Two of the most prominent individuals who sounded the alarm about not just the prospect but the virtually inevitable reality of a pandemic were Microsoft CEO Bill Gates (2020) and— decades earlier—the well-respected analysis from a leading science writer Laurie Garrett (1994). In fact, just months before the dawn of Covid, in March 2019, the World Health Organization (WHO) warned of the possibility of a sudden flu pandemic in the coming years (Saplakoglu, 2019).

However, much of the following analysis focuses on the troublesome American political response—with a particular emphasis on some key decisions from the Trump administration. Ghitis (2021) argued that other world leaders with similar (or even greater) shades of populism or authoritarianism exhibited behaviors that proved to be fairly devastating for their respective populations. A particularly glaring example may be the case of Brazilian President Jair Bolsonaro whose nation (as of late 2021) was only second to the United States in terms of its total Covid deaths. During the height of the pandemic, not only did Bolsonaro (who contracted Covid himself) flagrantly ignore any protective measures about the virus but also told his citizenry to "stop whining" about the virus, which he likened to "little flu." While the pandemic raises important philosophical and legal questions about the boundaries between governmental mandates and personal rights, there is the concern that authoritarian leaders may strive to use the pandemic to their political advantage by further stifling debate and gaining greater power (Tuccille, 2020).

It is an understatement to further note that the pandemic has produced a profound shift in geopolitical relations and tensions. One such example often emphasized by the World Health Organization (WHO) is that wealthier countries have been stockpiling more vaccines than needed at the expense of poorer developing nations (Goldhill, 2021). Perhaps to underscore this point, the two particularly infectious Covid variants which became the predominant strains in the United States in mid-to-late 2021 originated in India (Delta) and Southern Africa (Omicron), respectively. And, related to this point was the fact that the United States initially employed a controversial travel ban for several South African countries as a means to curtail the spread of the Omicron variant—though this was criticized on the basis that not only was this decision not rooted in science but it only served as a punitive effect against countries (like South Africa) that provided scientific knowledge and warning of this new variant (Serino, 2021).

One of the greatest geopolitical consequences may be the relationship that China has with the United States. Even prior to the pandemic, Americans had growing concerns over economic policies and human rights with respect to China—though the pandemic has further strained these relations (Hass, 2021). Interestingly, at the start of the pandemic, both the scientific and journalistic communities widely believed that the likely source of the virus was from an animal—a bat—that may have been further exposed to another animal sold at a wet market in Wuhan, China in December 2019 (Maxmen, 2021). However, in early-to-mid 2021, there was a growing scientific debate over a hypothesis that was initially controversial (if not somewhat conspiratorial) at the start of the pandemic—that is, the virus may have somehow escaped as a lab leak from the Wuhan Institute of Virology—though the initial wet market theory remains quite plausible, the lab leak hypothesis has been shown to be at least a possibility (Maxmen & Mallapaty, 2021). Indeed, a 90-day investigation by the Biden administration that was publicly released in late August 2021 noted inconclusive evidence about Covid's origins, but the report stated:

> Beijing, however, continues to hinder the global investigation, resist sharing information and blame other countries, including the United States...These actions reflect, in part, China's government's own uncertainty about where the investigation could lead as well as its frustration the international community is using the issue to exert political pressure on China (Ward, 2021, p. 1).

This report highlights a portion of the social psychological definition of conflict where there are at least two parties with perceived differing goals or interests; though, thus far, there has not been a clear or direct action against China, which is the second key component of conflict (Bar-Tal, 2011). Given the very profound interdependence that China and the United States share, despite these tensions, it would seem difficult to imagine a deeper conflict between these countries over the pandemic and its origins (Hass, 2021).

An American Disaster: The Political Response

In my initial planning of this book, this chapter was intended to be included towards the end of this book. Given the tragic way the pandemic has been politicized, the importance of key political considerations has been moved to the forefront of this book. In fact, it is widely believed that the poor and dysfunctional political climate coupled with a rushed desire to reopen the economy (especially in the early months of the pandemic) and insufficient funding for public health all created the uniquely disastrous American response (Achenbach et al., 2020). As to truly highlight this point, Anthony Fauci remarked in July 2021 that the United States may still have currently been facing polio and smallpox outbreaks if the same levels of anti-vaccination resistance had been present when the vaccines for these respective viruses were released (Schnell, 2021).

However, this book strives to take an apolitical tone in evaluating some of the key political decisions and impacts associated with the pandemic insomuch that weaknesses of both American political parties are considered. This goal notwithstanding, naturally, readers of this book may form their own views as to whether, as the author, I have conducted this analysis with a particular political bias. Let us begin this critique by first noting that many significant blunders occurred by and from more left of center political leaders. California's governor, Gavin Newsom, faced an unsuccessful recall election largely spurred by pushback against his very aggressive mitigation efforts along with a well-publicized incident where he was dining maskless with a group of friends and lobbyists at an expensive restaurant (Ronayne, 2021). In New York alone, there are at least three glaring such examples. Oxiris Barbot, who was the New York City Commissioner of Health at the time of the start of the pandemic declared in early February 2020: "this is not something that you're going to contract in the subway or the bus" (Goodman, 2020, p. 7) and further stated that Covid "is not an illness that can be easily spread through casual contact" (Associated Press, 2020, p. 7). Barbot, who resigned from her position in August 2020 and later suggested that many of her warnings of the imminent threat of the pandemic were not fully heeded, would later criticize many of the actions of then-New York City Mayor Bill de Blasio during the early weeks and months of the pandemic such as his policies of housing and then removing the homeless from various city hotels (Sommerfeldt, 2021). Indeed, de Blasio had faced a wide array of criticisms from the pandemic, including (but not limited to) a slow response to reacting to the pandemic (including closing public schools) to calling out the Jewish community for large gatherings in defiance of social distancing mandates (Raymond, 2020). Despite their shared political party, de Blasio had long been at odds with the then-Governor of New York, Andrew Cuomo, at the time of the pandemic (Goodman, 2020). In the immediate weeks and months of the start of the pandemic, Cuomo was lavishly praised for his widely perceived calm and steady leadership; further, his daily news briefings initially won him an Emmy and he authored a book on how he faced the pandemic crisis. In an incredible twist of fate, all of this glory was abruptly halted when Cuomo resigned as New York Governor in August 2021 following an extensive New York State investigation involving several sexual harassment allegations; his leadership was further tarnished over questions about how Covid-related nursing home deaths were potentially underreported in New York (Goldmacher, 2021).

Key Trump Administration and Republican Actions and Beliefs

This analysis does not at all presume or try to make the case that all Republican officials perpetuated poor decisions during the pandemic—in fact, several Republican governors, such as Ohio's Mike DeWine and Maryland's Larry Hogan, were widely praised for their attentive and focused realization of the threat posed by the pandemic (e.g., Scher, 2020). Yet, many Republican governors—notably, Florida's Ron DeSantis and Texas' Greg Abbott—sought to flaunt their opposition to mask and vaccine mandates to perhaps appease their right-wing base (Smith & Levin, 2021). Just like the Covid pandemic, the 1918 pandemic found that cities that emphasized mask-wearing and discouraged mass gatherings tended to reduce infections and deaths (Markel, 2020). And, governors who did implement suggestions from public health officials—like Pennsylvania's Tom Wolf—were often derided by political adversaries, where impeachment attempts occurred (Gibson, 2020). Arguably more troubling though were some political statements that were often viewed as wrong-headed or even callous such as Missouri Governor Mike Parson's view that if children get Covid they would just "get over it" (Beer, 2020) or the Texas lieutenant governor's view that was widely interpreted as an insensitive implication that it was critical to ensure the reopening of the economy even if it meant not taking steps that could have particularly endangered the elderly (Rodriguez, 2020).

United States President Harry S. Truman and his famous "The Buck Stops Here" desk sign emphasized the unique and oversized role that the leader of the American executive branch has in shaping or effecting public policy. Imagine a President who purposefully downplayed the gravity of a spreading disease—and likely helped to advance its spread—while becoming infected with the disease himself. While reading this statement, perhaps you imagined Donald Trump in his handling of the coronavirus pandemic (e.g., Mason & Barabak, 2020). But, here, I am actually referring to the Democratic President Woodrow Wilson who was the commander-in-chief during the most devastating pandemic prior to Covid—that is, the 1918 influenza pandemic. Like Trump, Wilson was not forthcoming about his contracting the virus and he did little to curtail its spread; if anything, the push to win World War I may have contributed to its proliferation (Davis, 2018; Barry, 2005).

Shifting from the pandemic of Wilson's era to Covid, the egregious blunders from the Trump administration—with a particular focus on Donald Trump himself—have been well articulated and argued from virtually every phase of the pandemic so much so that the pandemic has been described as the worst intelligence failure in American history (largely due to Trump's leadership; Zenko, 2020). Well before the pandemic, there were several analyses and reports that (at the very least) seriously questioned the leadership and goals of the Trump administration—including Trump himself (e.g., Nance, 2019). From the beginning, there was a sense that the Trump administration severely downplayed or overlooked the Covid threat by often expecting overwhelmed State governments to find their own solutions and questionable actions of when and for whom travel—particularly international travel—was permitted to the United States (Shear et al., 2020). For instance, there was much focus on travel emanating from China, in particular, in the early months of the pandemic but much less on Europe; and, Trump himself made many spurious claims that the virus would somehow miraculously disappear in late February 2020 as well as the particularly infamous (and dangerous) suggestion at an April 2020 news conference where he pondered whether bleach could be used somehow as an internal disinfectant of the virus (e.g., Yong, 2020). But, as the pandemic persisted into summer 2020, Trump and his aides carried out actions that arguably worsened the situation, including retweeting anti-masking sentiments (Robin, 2020) and hosting political rallies that put individuals at risk for contracting the virus (Contreras, 2020). For instance, then White House chief of staff Mark Meadows reportedly would only selectively hold Covid update meetings with like-minded staff while questioning public health and scientific protocols (such as mask-wearing) and admonishing health leaders like Anthony Fauci or Deborah Birx for veering off message; all the while, Donald Trump would turn to Twitter to stoke messages that could—at the very least—be incendiary to many and potentially undermine or ignore public health messages or concerns such as an early August 2020 Tweet of "OPEN THE SCHOOLS!!!" (Rucker et al., 2020). The latter inflammatory Trump tweet was consistent with earlier April 2020 Tweets where in three successive posts he wrote "LIBERATE

MINNESOTA!," "LIBERATE MICHIGAN!", and "LIBERATE VIRGINIA, and save your great 2nd Amendment. It is under siege!" While it is impossible to know with any certainty what precisely Donald Trump was thinking while composing those Tweets, it is widely believed that they were aimed at—just a month or so following his own declaration of a national emergency—that (the then) Democratic governors of these States abandon Covid mitigation efforts. And, quite disturbingly, one of the governors indirectly alluded to—(then) Michigan Governor Gretchen Whitmer—was targeted in a kidnapping plot by a right-wing Michigan militia group because of these very lockdowns (Roche, 2020).

Dr. Anthony Fauci, director of the National Institute of Allergy and Infectious Diseases, was a notable figure in the Trump White House Coronavirus Task Force for voicing his concerns fairly openly (and purportedly against pressures from some in the Trump administration; Axelrod, 2021). As an example of his frankness, in June 2020, he described Covid as his "worst nightmare" due to the fact that it was a highly transmissible respiratory infection that likely originated from an animal; this was in contrast to a virus like Ebola, which he termed "scary" but did not spread easily or HIV which was more drawn out as a crisis and the initial outbreak threat in the 1980s was often perceived as being relegated to select populations (Christensen, 2020). However, for as much praise as Fauci has received, some have criticized his supposed downplaying of the threat prior to March 2020, including not initially recommending masks (though he would later suggest that was done to avoid a run on them and to ensure that health care workers would have an adequate supply; D. Wallace-Wells, 2021). About a month after Trump left office, Fauci would later bemoan the political divisiveness regarding much of the former President's actions. In particular, when asked by a CNN reporter about whether Trump's "denial and lack of facts contributed to this level of loss," Fauci responded:

> I'm uncomfortable going back and directly criticizing, but it's really almost self evident that when you're trying to signal the country to really buckle down and address the kinds of mitigation strategies that we put forth — the wearing of masks, the physical distancing, the avoiding congregate settings, the kinds of things that I and many of the other public health people, who were there, trying to get the country to appreciate the this that we were trying to do all throughout the entire outbreak. I mean, the thing that I remember very clearly is when we were trying to open up the country, open up the economy and to do it carefully with the gateway, the phase 1, phase 2, the phase 3. I was hoping that would see a uniform, unified approach towards all doing that together. And when signals come saying 'this isn't so bad, we're in pretty good shape,' when we're saying we're not, we being the health

people, that was not helpful, because the people who wanted to deny that this is something that was serious when you get a signal from above that it might not be [so bad], then you don't do the kinds of things you need to do (Meyer, 2021, pp. 2-3).

Dr. Deborah Birx, who worked with Dr. Fauci to manage the Trump White House pandemic response, in late January 2021, voiced similarly restrained criticism for Donald Trump and his administration but also some degree of frustration that the then-President was receiving questionable data and information that she did not personally create or even know the precise source (Newburger, 2021).

Dr. Rochelle Walensky, who was named director of the U.S. Centers for Disease Control and Prevention (CDC) by President Joseph Biden in 2021, helped to lead a review of some of the agency's guidance during the Trump administration and found many claims not rooted in science. Perhaps even more concerning were claims that important information was being withheld from the public, such as then-CDC official Dr. Nancy Messonnier's unheeded warning that the virus was likely to bring severe disruption to American life and necessary preparations were required (Bonifield et al., 2021). In fact, in June 2020 testimony to Congress, then-CDC director Robert Redfield stated that "We lost the containment edge" (Vergano & Hirji, 2020). In a telling 2018 blog post published by the CDC to commemorate the one-hundred anniversary of the 1918 flu pandemic, this blog remains an astounding critique of the CDC with a bit of hindsight in that it discussed how that particular virus spread quickly and overwhelmed the health care system but yet the "CDC works tirelessly to protect Americans and the global community from the threat of a future flu pandemic" (CDC Blog Administrator, 2018, p. 3).

The Early Biden Pandemic Response: Promise and Pitfalls

Perhaps somewhat surprisingly, the Covid crisis was only the third-most greatest factor in voters' decisions for president according to 2020 Election Day exit polls (ranked behind the economy and racial inequality). However, 52% of that sample felt that controlling the pandemic was more important even if it hurt the economy; such voters tended to overwhelmingly support the then-Democratic candidate Joseph Biden (Miao, 2020). Biden assumed the presidency under rather inauspicious circumstances on January 20, 2021—just two weeks following the Capitol riots with the expected winter Covid surge occurring with scant few Americans vaccinated at that point. However, he came into office largely receiving high praise from public health officials given his strong focus on not just trying to get the pandemic under some control but also with respect to his fervent belief to listen to advice and information from credible scientific officials (Siemaszko, 2021). Even though there was some public discontent over the difficulty for many in securing a vaccine in the first months of its availability (Miao, 2021), by late April 2021, all American adults were eligible for a Covid vaccine and there was general, ample availability by that point (Mundell, 2021).

Biden himself portrayed a public sense that Americans now had a very real chance to have a "summer of freedom" from the virus on June 2, 2021 (B. Wallace-Wells, 2021). Around this same time period, the CDC made what is now largely viewed as a major blunder—after initially suggesting that vaccinated individuals would not necessarily need to wear masks, it reversed itself about a month later in late May 2021 as the Delta variant started to surge in America; this decision arguably only further eroded trust in the CDC and potentially the Biden administration as well (Karan, 2021). Further tensions and confusion between the Biden administration and the CDC developed in early autumn 2021 when there were conflicting messages about when and for whom a booster shot would be available or necessary (Banco et al., 2021). And, during the height of the Omicron surge, it was commonly remarked at how dumbfounded it was that basic Covid testing was again a challenge for many (Collinson, 2021).

Just as it would be unfair to absolutely reject all actions of the Trump administration—after all, the vaccine was developed during the latter part of this term—in many respects, it may be unfair to absolutely criticize Biden and his administration for these actions largely committed during the second-half of his first year in office. The virus itself and the science of the pandemic continues to evolve—and, with it, new information can potentially be modified accordingly. However, the Biden administration should have been mindful of the importance of persuasion-based messages and techniques particularly with respect to maintaining a consistent, credible message especially given that about half of America is likely to not be that receptive to the messaging in the first place (Benoit & Benoit, 2008). Perhaps it was naïve or overly optimistic to have stated that Americans could achieve "independence" from the virus by presuming that virtually all Americans would get vaccinated. After a year in office, the Biden administration shifted its strategy to reframe this issue by suggesting that Covid is likely to remain part of everyday life (Siddiqui, 2022). As pessimistic of a message as that may sound, perhaps such candor and acknowledgments at the start of his term would have been more appropriate.

Most significant world or historical events can always be looked through the prism of hindsight and what could or should have been. For instance, Franklin Delano Roosevelt is often criticized for not necessarily doing enough to help European Jews during the period of the Holocaust—even though, at that time, he subtly pursued many policies and actions that were helpful (e.g., Medoff, 2013). We could certainly entertain whether any individual of any political party would have been perfectly equipped to address the threat that the pandemic represented. Further, the pandemic response did not merely necessarily involve one particular failure from one particular person—there were a panoply of failures across many agencies and institutions. Perhaps what should concern us is best summarized by President Abraham Lincoln's famous quote in his "House Divided" speech where he opined that "A house divided against itself cannot stand." America is a country where some fervently believe that Covid mitigation measures were either unnecessary or an abomination; others believe that they were absolutely necessary and perhaps did not go far enough. Quite troublingly, some of these political differences may have even obscured a recognition and realization of the grief that so many have experienced in the pandemic (as discussed further in Chapter 5; Graff, 2020). While it is debatable (and even questionable) whether the pandemic directly created these political divides, it has arguably worsened them.

References

Achenbach, J., Wan, W., Brulliard, K., & Janes, C., (2020, July 19). The crisis that shocked the world: America's response to the coronavirus. *Washington Post.* https://www.washingtonpost.com/health/2020/07/19/coronavirus-us-failure/

Associated Press. (2020, March 2). Officials try to calm nerves as NY reports 1st COVID-19 case. *AP.* https://apnews.com/article/6b9d9bf2f753ba7944c4dac379b3c5bb

Axelrod, T. (2021, January 23). Fauci describes 'chilling' pressure on scientists in Trump era. *The Hill.* https://thehill.com/policy/healthcare/535515-fauci-describes-chilling-pressure-on-scientists-in-trump-era

Banco, E., Owermohle, S., & Cancryn, A. (2021, September 13). Tensions mount between CDC and Biden health team over boosters. *Politico.* https://www.politico.com/news/2021/09/13/cdc-biden-health-team-vaccine-boosters-511529

Bar-Tal, D. (2011). Introduction: Conflicts and social psychology. In D. Bar-Tal (Ed.) *Intergroup conflicts and their resolution: Social psychological perspective* (pp. 1-38). Taylor & Francis/Psychology Press.

Barry, J. M. (2005). *The great influenza: The epic story of the deadliest plague in history.* Penguin Books.

Beer, T. (2020, July 20). Missouri governor says kids will get coronavirus in schools, but 'they're going to get over it'. *Forbes.* https://www.forbes.com/sites/tommybeer/2020/07/20/missouri-governor-says-kids-will-get-coronavirus-in-schools-but-theyre-going-to-get-over-it

Benoit, W. L., & Benoit, P. J. (2008). *Persuasive messages: The process of influence.* Blackwell Publishing.

Bonifield, J., Howard, J., & Kelly, C. (2021, March 15). Agency review finds some Trump administration CDC guidance was not grounded in science or free from undue influence. *CNN.* https://www.cnn.com/2021/03/15/politics/cdc-guidance-trump-administration-review/index.html

CDC Blog Administrator. (2018, May 14). The 1918 flu pandemic: Why it matters 100 years later. *CDC.* https://blogs.cdc.gov/publichealthmatters/2018/05/1918-flu/

Christensen, J. (2020, June 9). Ebola was "scary," HIV was "insidiously" spread, but Covid-19 is Fauci's "worst nightmare." *CNN.* https://www.cnn.com/world/live-news/coronavirus-pandemic-06-09-20-intl/h_686274668754c93dd5a3ccafcdf33e8a

Collinson, S. (2021, December 28). Biden grapples with a Covid-19 testing failure that could have been foreseen. *CNN.* https://edition.cnn.com/2021/12/28/politics/joe-biden-covid-19-testing-failure/index.html

Contreras, G. W. (2020, June 20). The Trump rally in Tulsa is a recipe for disaster. *STAT.* https://www.statnews.com/2020/06/20/trump-rally-tulsa-recipe-for-disaster/

Davis, K. C. (2018). *More deadly than war: The hidden history of the Spanish Flu and the First World War.* Henry Holt and Company.

Garrett, L. (1994). *The coming plague: Newly emerging diseases in a world out of balance.* Penguin.

Gates, B. (2020). Responding to Covid-19—A once-in-a-century pandemic? *The New England Journal of Medicine, 382*(18), 1677–1679. https://doi.org/10.1056/NEJMp2003762

Ghitis, F. (2021, March 30). Which world leader has the worst pandemic record? The competition is fierce. *Washington Post.* https://www.washingtonpost.com/opinions/2021/03/30/which-world-leader-has-worst-pandemic-record-competition-is-fierce/

Gibson, B. (2020, June 16). Rep. Daryl Metcalfe reveals 5 articles of impeachment against Gov. Tom Wolf. *TribLive.* https://triblive.com/news/pennsylvania/rep-daryl-metcalfe-reveals-5-articles-of-impeachment-against-gov-tom-wolf/

Goldhill, O. (2021, December 13). We have enough Covid vaccines for most of the world. But rich countries are stockpiling more than they need for boosters. *STAT.* https://www.statnews.com/2021/12/13/we-have-enough-covid-vaccines-for-most-of-world-but-rich-countries-stockpiling-more-than-they-need/

Goldmacher, S. (2021, March 13/November 10). The imperious rise and accelerating fall of Andrew Cuomo. *The New York Times.* https://www.nytimes.com/2021/03/13/us/politics/andrew-cuomo-scandals.html

Goodman, J. D. (2020, April 8/July 18). How delays and unheeded warnings hindered New York's virus fight. *The New York Times.* https://www.nytimes.com/2020/04/08/nyregion/new-york-coronavirus-response-delays.html

Graff, G. M. (2020, September 10). The grief Americans no longer share. *The Atlantic.* https://www.theatlantic.com/ideas/archive/2020/09/america-loses-its-capacity-common-grief/616234/

Hass, R. (2021, August 12). The "new normal" in US-China relations: Hardening competition and deep interdependence. *Brookings.* https://www.brookings.edu/blog/order-from-chaos/2021/08/12/the-new-normal-in-us-china-relations-hardening-competition-and-deep-interdependence/

Karan, A. (2021, May 27). The CDC's latest blunder is really about trust, not masks. *STAT.* https://www.statnews.com/2021/05/27/cdc-latest-blunder-about-trust-not-masks/

Markel, H. (2020, May 31). Pandemic historian: Don't rush reopening. In 1918, some states ran straight into more death. *USA Today.* https://www.usatoday.com/story/opinion/2020/05/31/lessons-1918-flu-coronavirus-social-distancing-historian-column/5283023002/

Mason, M., & Barabak, M. Z. (2020, October 4). News analysis: A history of falsehoods comes back to haunt the COVID-stricken president. *Los Angeles Times.* https://www.latimes.com/politics/story/2020-10-04/trump-coronavirus-diagnosis-trust

Maxmen, A. (2021). WHO report into COVID pandemic origins zeroes in on animal markets, not labs. *Nature, 592,* 173-174. https://doi.org/10.1038/d415 86-021-00865-8

Maxmen, A., & Mallapaty, S. (2021). The COVID lab-leak hypothesis: what scientists do and don't know. *Nature, 594,* 313-315. https://doi.org/10.1038/d41586-021-01529-3

Medoff, R. (2013). *FDR and the Holocaust: A breach of faith.* The David S. Wyman Institute for Holocaust Studies.

Meyer, K. (2021, February 15). Dr. Fauci Says Trump's 'denial and lack of facts' contributed to magnitude of U.S. Covid death toll. *Mediaite.* https://www.mediaite.com/tv/dr-fauci-says-trumps-denial-and-lack-of-facts-contributed-to-magnitude-of-u-s-covid-death-toll/

Miao, H. (2020, November 3). Here's what mattered most to voters in the 2020 election, according to exit poll. *CNBC.* https://www.cnbc.com/2020/11/03/exit-polls-heres-what-mattered-most-to-voters-in-the-2020-election.html

Miao, H. (2021, January 21). Americans grow more optimistic about Covid but blame feds for rocky vaccine rollout, NBC News poll says. *CNBC.* https://www.cnbc.com/2021/01/21/voters-more-optimistic-about-covid-blame-feds-for-vaccine-rollout-nbc-poll.html

Mundell, E. (2021, April 20). Every American adult now eligible for COVID-19 vaccine. *US News & World Report.* https://www.usnews.com/news/health-news/articles/2021-04-20/every-american-adult-now-eligible-for-covid-19-vaccine

Nance, M. W. (2019). *The plot to betray America: How Team Trump embraced our enemies, compromised our security, and how we can fix it.* Hachette Books.

Newburger, E. (2021, January 24). Birx says someone was giving Trump 'parallel data' about Covid pandemic. *CNBC.* https://www.cnbc.com/2021/01/24/birx-says-someone-was-giving-trump-parallel-data-about-covid-pandemic.html

Raymond, A. K. (2020, April 29). De Blasio blasted for calling out 'Jewish community' after crowded funeral. *Intelligencer.* https://nymag.com/intelligencer/2020/04/de-blasio-blasted-for-criticism-of-crowded-orthodox-funeral.html

Robin, J. (2020, June 24). The new mask fight exposes an old American divide. *NY1.* https://www.ny1.com/nyc/all-boroughs/news/2020/06/24/as-mask-mandates-return--so-does-the-debate-over-rights

Roche, D. (2020, October 9). Fact-check: Did Trump's 'Liberate Michigan' Tweet inspire plot to kidnap Gov. Whitmer? *Newsweek.* https://www.newsweek.com/

donald-trump-liberate-michigan-tweet-plot-kidnap-gretchen-whitmer-governor-1537719

Rodriguez, A. (2020, March 24). Texas' lieutenant governor suggests grandparents are willing to die for US economy. *USA Today*. https://www.usatoday.com/story/news/nation/2020/03/24/covid-19-texas-official-suggests-elderly-willing-die-economy/2905990001/

Ronayne, K. (2021, September 8). Newsom's nightmare: How one November day fueled the recall. *AP News*. https://apnews.com/article/entertainment-health-elections-california-coronavirus-pandemic-c4cbdfdfa832495d19b4c1639f1cfb90

Rucker, P. Abutaleb, Y. Dawsey, J., & Costa, R. (2020, August 8). The lost days of summer: How Trump fell short in containing the virus. *The Washington Post*. https://www.washingtonpost.com/politics/trump-struggled-summer-coronavirus/2020/08/08/e12ceace-d80a-11ea-aff6-220dd3a14741_story.html

Saplakoglu, Y. (2019, March 14). We're due for a flu pandemic. How will it start? *Live Science*. https://www.livescience.com/64992-how-flu-becomes-pandemic.html

Scher, B. (2020, April 1). Coronavirus vs. governors: Ranking the best and worst state leaders. *Politico*. https://www.politico.com/news/magazine/2020/04/01/coronavirus-state-governors-best-worst-covid-19-159945

Schnell, M. (2021, July 18). Fauci: Smallpox wouldn't have been eradicated with today's 'false information'. *The Hill*. https://thehill.com/policy/healthcare/563567-fauci-smallpox-polio-would-still-be-in-us-if-todays-false-information-was

Serino, K. (2021, December 2). Travel bans punish countries for doing necessary work to end the pandemic, South Africa epidemiologist says. *PBS*. https://www.pbs.org/newshour/health/outrageous-and-an-overreaction-south-africas-top-epidemiologist-responds-to-omicron-travel-ban

Shear, M. D., Weiland, N., Lipton, E., Haberman, M., & Sanger, D. E. (2020, July 18). Inside Trump's failure: The rush to abandon leadership role on the virus. *The New York Times*. https://www.nytimes.com/2020/07/18/us/politics/trump-coronavirus-response-failure-leadership.html

Sommerfeldt, C. (2021, July 26). NYC Mayor de Blasio's ex-health czar says he'd put 'entire city' at risk of COVID by booting homeless from hotels. *New York Daily News*. https://www.nydailynews.com/news/politics/new-york-elections-government/ny-de-blasio-ex-health-commissioner-dangerous-plan-homeless-hotels-20210726-ajitlcuzobednbrfoobt6p2ocy-story.html

Siddiqui, S. (2022, January 6). Biden, in shift, prepares Americans to see Covid-19 as part of life. *The Wall Street Journal*. https://www.wsj.com/articles/biden-in-shift-prepares-americans-to-see-covid-19-as-part-of-life-11641465004

Siemaszko, C. (2021, January 21). Experts praise Biden's Covid-19 plan, but warn that undoing Trump-era mistakes will take time. *NBC News*. https://www.nbcnews.com/news/us-news/experts-praise-biden-s-covid-19-plan-warn-undoing-trump-n1255210

Smith, M., & Levin, J. (2021, October 16). Republican governor 'frenemies' compete for national limelight. *Bloomberg*. https://www.bloombergquint.com/onweb/republican-governor-frenemies-compete-for-national-limelight

Tuccille, J. D. (2020, October 5). The post-pandemic 'new normal' looks awfully authoritarian. *Reason*. https://reason.com/2020/10/05/the-post-pandemic-new-normal-looks-awfully-authoritarian/

Vergano, D., & Hirji, Z. (2020, June 24). The CDC lost control of the coronavirus pandemic. Then the agency disappeared. *BuzzFeed News.* https://www.buzz feednews.com/article/danvergano/cdc-coronavirus-containment-redfield

Wallace-Wells, B. (2021, August 12). What happened to Joe Biden's "summer of freedom" from the pandemic? *The New Yorker.* https://www.newyorker.com/news/annals-of-inquiry/what-happened-to-joe-bidens-summer-of-freedom-from-the-pandemic

Wallace-Wells, D. (2021, March 15). How the West lost COVID. *Intelligencer.* https://nymag.com/intelligencer/2021/03/how-the-west-lost-covid-19.html

Ward, M. (2021, August 27). Covid-19 origins still murky after Biden administration's 90-day investigation. *Politico.* https://www.politico.com/news/2021/08/27/covid-origins-biden-investigation-507014

Yong, E. (2020, August 4). How the pandemic defeated America. *The Atlantic.* https://www.theatlantic.com/magazine/archive/2020/09/coronavirus-american-failure/614191/

Zenko, M. (2020, March 25). The coronavirus is the worst intelligence failure in U.S. history. *FP.* https://foreignpolicy.com/2020/03/25/coronavirus-worst-intelligence-failure-us-history-covid-19/

CHAPTER THREE

Economic Fears and Threats

This chapter considers some of the economic losses associated with the pandemic as well as the related issues of how to weigh economic versus health concerns and some of the threats posed by an unstable economy. Indeed, the pandemic has severely disrupted workforces across the economy, including the ways and means of how products are manufactured and consumed (Nicola et al., 2020).

While the precise estimates vary somewhat as a function of when a given poll was taken and by whom, separate worldwide polls conducted by U.S. management consultants McKinsey and PwC taken in spring 2022 suggest that around two-fifths of workers were unhappy with their jobs and thinking about leaving (Ellerbeck, 2022). The so-called "Great Resignation" has, at least for a time post-pandemic, become a reality as the U.S. "quit rate" reached a 20-year high in November 2021 (Parker & Horowitz, 2022). As an example of such experiences, Emory University business professor Tom Smith suggests that many workers are thinking "[I'm] done with a cubicle. I'm done with commuting. I'm done sitting in an office" and further adds the vast challenges associated with the pandemic entailed "Maybe the looking at the craziness in the eye and coming out on the other end made people re-evaluate how much risk is actually involved [in changing their job]" (Strassmann, 2021, p. 1). Further, a Pew Research Center survey found that, compared with a nationally representative sample of U.S. adults from September 2017, the percentage of adults who stated that their job, occupation, or career brought a sense of meaning declined from 24% to 17% in February 2021 (Van Kessel & Silver, 2021). Though leaving one's job may be unrealistic or impossible for many, some are striving for an earlier than expected retirement or at least a job that provides a better fit or greater work-life balance (Vasel, 2021).

Weighing Economic versus Health Concerns

Forslid and Herzing (2021) argue that there is a tradeoff between economic costs to a society and health outcomes in a pandemic such that longer quarantines—even if they help to curtail the spread of a virus like Covid—also imply larger economic losses. Trying to successfully find and navigate a way to keep people safe from the virus while not eviscerating jobs and the economy has been a central concern from the earliest days of the pandemic. As an example, another academic analysis from Li et al. (2022) found that States with increasingly stricter social distancing protocols from June to August 2020 were associated with improved outcomes (e.g., fewer death rates) in nursing homes. Even though the previous chapter explored the basic political paradigm underlying the pandemic, it is virtually impossible to ignore these political effects in this section (and, indeed, throughout this book)—particularly since governmental and other leaders have had to try to weigh this delicate balance. Despite warnings from Dr. Anthony Fauci, the desire to start to reopen sectors of the American economy was already becoming palpable as early as late April 2020 with many States, like Georgia, criticized at the time for allowing less critical businesses to reopen like bowling alleys and beauty parlors (James, 2020). As the initial Covid wave seemed to slow in early May 2020, it was becoming increasingly clear that the warmth of the summer would not halt the spread of the virus. This time though, much of the focus in the spread of the virus started to shift to areas of the country (particularly the South) that were first not as impacted—and, around that time, principal deputy director of the CDC, Dr. Anne Schuchat conceded "We have way too much virus across the country" particularly in contrast to other areas like "New Zealand or Singapore or Korea where a new case is rapidly identified and all the contacts are traced and people are isolated who are sick and people who are exposed are quarantined" (Feuer, 2020, p. 2).

Though many State-imposed mandates were lifted just weeks into the pandemic, during the summer 2021 Delta surge, when vaccines were widely available, Wu (2021) reminded us that indoor mask-wearing still was prudent given that the vaccines were not perfectly foolproof and they still offered protection to oneself and others; she further added they didn't pose much of burden to wear either. In mid-December 2021, it was reported that only nine States had (or reimposed) some sort of mask mandate just as the Omicron surge was beginning to take hold—though well before this point, many State legislators removed any legal authority for governors to impose such mandates again (Simmons-Duffin, 2021).

The Pushback: Disturbing Trends Against Stay at Home and Mask Orders

As previously noted, in many States and jurisdictions, any form of health mitigation strategy was completely lifted—in some cases, just weeks after Donald Trump's mid-March 2020 national emergency declaration. Many governors who once imposed mask mandates, like Pennsylvania's then-Governor Tom Wolf (who encouraged mask-wearing following the Delta summer 2021 surge), did not (or could not) mandate them again (Associated Press, 2021). Such decisions often left schools and businesses in a quandary of sorts regarding how or whether to impose such mandates themselves. While businesses cannot largely mandate their customers to follow mitigation policies or be vaccinated, the Supreme Court upheld school and university vaccine mandates (R. Barnes, 2021) while blocking mandates (supported by the Biden administration) for large private businesses (though allowing them for medical facilities that receive Medicare or Medicaid payments; Breuninger & Kimball, 2022).

Halverson et al. (2021) detailed how science and public health became so political during the pandemic that the recommendations of state and local health officials were often severely undermined by public opinion, even if the advised protective health measures were objectively sound. Tragically though, many public health officials were relentlessly attacked and received death threats, so much so that dozens had resigned or been fired in the first few months of the pandemic, where many of the incendiary comments featured vicious and hateful language (Mello et al., 2020) including sexist, anti-Semitic, or transphobic overtones (Deliso, 2020).

Ward et al. (2022) conducted a fairly comprehensive mixed-methods study of the National Association of County and City Health Officials' (NACCHO) full census of 2,430 local health departments and found that harassment occurred in 57% of these departments during the early months of the pandemic. Between March 2020 to January 2021, these researchers also noted 256 cases of health department officials who left their position with nearly two-thirds representing resignations or retirements (and only 20 outright firings). While it might be expected that the public health workers who were fired rather than quit represent a conceptual difference, Ward et al. (2022) tended to blur any such differences; rather, they highlighted that these individuals faced much harassment (including threats both online and at home) and much burnout. Much of this pressure was also due to the fact that such officials often report to other elected officials, boards of health, and groups who may have their own personal or political agendas that may not necessarily align with that of health department leaders (Kounang, 2021). Just as concerning was a finding from a survey (using NORC's AmeriSpeak Panel) of 1,086 U.S. adults, which found that harassing or threatening public health officials because of business closures was justified rose from 20% to 25% and 15% to 21%, respectively from November 2020 to July and August 2021 (such that those with lower income and education were more likely to support such views; Topazian et al., 2022).

Like public health officials, school board members and associated school staff have also received some of the same hateful vitriol—again, often injected with sexist, racist, or anti-Semitic slurs (Hanna, 2021). According to an Edweek Research Center survey from November 2021, 60% of principals and district leaders who replied said at least one of their staff members had faced threats from individuals upset over Covid-related protocols like mask-wearing or social distancing (Kurtz, 2021). To a certain extent, these incendiary actions may have reflected anti-science sentiments (Kretchmar & Brewer, 2022), but it also reflects how toxic political debates have been permeating into public school curriculum discussions (Sawchuk, 2021). As to further highlight the dysfunctional American political response, the United States Justice Department was criticized by many Republican lawmakers when it announced it would evaluate threats against educators (Atterbury & Perez, 2021), including a lawsuit from some parents who largely viewed those actions as a violation of free speech; though the outcomes from the U.S. Department of Justice were unknown at the time of this writing, a federal judge threw out the aforementioned lawsuit (Rabinowitz, 2022).

To offer some brief historical perspective, it is important to consider that there were often protests and defiance against mask mandates and other related ordinances during the 1918 influenza pandemic in America (Duncan, 2020). And, in the 1980s, Indiana teenager Ryan White became well known after he was diagnosed with AIDS following a blood transfusion—and then later initially prevented by his high school (and further shunned by other parents) from attending public school. In a sad twist of fate, his case received additional attention in November 2021 when a conservative commentator seemed to liken how non-vaccinated people were treated as those affected by the AIDS crisis; many critics responded by highlighting the overt discrimination experienced by Ryan White (Kim, 2021). In short, there are at least some historical antecedents involving pushback or even antisocial behavior when faced with a new public health threat or challenge.

An Unstable Economy and Links to Broader Societal Concerns

The American and world economy has been severely challenged since the start of the pandemic (which was even further challenged with massive social justice movements and protests following the death of George Floyd; Wall Street Journal, 2020). Lowrey (2020) highlighted the rocky road to economic recovery by noting that many Americans were dependent on finite governmental stimulus funds (with state budgets being particularly tested) all the while many businesses were hurting from decreased demand.

Food and related supply chains have been greatly effected due to, initially, a changed demand in terms of the types of products that were being consumed (and where they were being consumed—increasingly, at home; Gasparro & Kang, 2020) to broader distribution and product availabilities in the latter part of 2021. In an eerie throwback to the start of the pandemic, in fall 2021, supply chain issues had again become increasingly problematic (Thompson, 2021). Like the start of the pandemic, it is not necessarily the case that there was panic buying per se but rather a host of factors that were slowing down (or preventing) manufacturers from dispensing their goods to customers (such as an inability to unload items at ports and a dearth of workers to transport them). In addition, bankruptcy protections rose 48% in May 2020 over the previous year (Brooks, 2020).

In an academic paper published in the early months of the pandemic, Van Bavel and colleagues (2020) reflected on much of the larger social and behavioral scientific literature to predict how the vast threat posed by the pandemic—beyond the virus itself—was a menace to society at large. Among their cited concerns were the risks of increased prejudice, the influence of social networks and changing social norms, the exploitation of social inequalities, cultural differences in response to the virus, and political polarizations. These scholars did not contend that these trends were inevitable or couldn't be used in a more prosocial way. For instance, social influences can certainly be used to promote healthful behavior and the greater good. Yet, they also cautioned how such influence could be used to peddle false information, including conspiracy theories. And, due to the unprecedented economic and social disruption created by the pandemic, the world is entering a transformative era ripe with the potential for great instability (Mead, 2020). As evidence of this point, the Federal Bureau of Investigation (FBI) reported that the U.S. murder rate was at its highest in over twenty years in 2020; though the precise causal factors remain unclear, economic strife, heightened stress, increased firearm purchases, and strained familial and community ties all likely contributed to this increase (King, 2021).

An even more shocking example representing a challenge to American democracy occurred when, in what should have been a fairly routine formality, on January 6, 2021, Congress was to convene to ratify and formally declare the winners of the 2020 American presidential contest, Joseph Biden and Kamala Harris. This date instead has gained a level of infamy in that it marks the first time in over 200 years—not since 1814 (as part of the War of 1812)—that the U.S. Congress was attacked; among other consequences, the alleged actions by Donald Trump of fairly steady stoking that Biden really was not the victor —in the weeks preceding it (after the 2020 winner was declared) and on that day itself—led to Trump's second impeachment trial in roughly a year (to which he was ultimately acquitted by the U.S. Senate lacking a two-thirds majority vote; Woodward & Costa, 2021). Trump's actions notwithstanding, it is widely believed that many extremist and militia groups (who were allegedly part of the Capitol riot) may have viewed their actions as justified, at least, in part, due to perceived angst or unfairness over Covid restrictions and related governmental conspiracy claims (which were often further amplified in online social media; Boone et al., 2021). There is evidence that pandemics have been associated with upending the political orthodoxy and many Americans feeling dismay or loneliness may latch onto extreme ideas in order to placate such feelings (Fisher, 2021). Historically, poorly handled disasters and crises are often ripe for extremist and even apocalyptic thinking where individuals see opportunities to radicalize or to act in more violent ways than they would have done under less stressful times (Jenkins, 2020).

A pair of surveys released days before the one-year anniversary of the Capitol attacks further underscored the grave concerns Americans had about their basic governance. In a NPR/Ispos poll conducted in late December 2021 with a sample of 1,126 American adults, 64% suggested that U.S. democracy was "in crisis and at risk of failing;" while Republicans were more likely to endorse this view than Democrats, they had different reasons for doing so—often rooted back to perceptions over the 2020 election and the January 6 riots (Rose & Baker, 2022). Another related troubling finding was that about a third of Americans—twice as many Republicans and Independents than Democrats— who felt that violence against the government was "sometimes justified" as reported by a Washington Post/University of Maryland poll also conducted in late December 2021 with 1,101 adults (Balz et al, 2022). Such findings are consistent with a 2021 Global Trends report produced by the U.S. National Intelligence Council, suggesting that the pandemic has fomented nationalism, strained governmental resources, and worsened economic inequalities (Tucker, 2021).

Further Changes in Economic Behavior

These serious aforesaid challenges notwithstanding, Mims (2020) contends that perhaps we should focus on the fact that the pandemic—aided by technology—has created a new "stay-at-home" economy for four basic reasons: companies have made great investments in quickly delivering goods and services to the home, families have invested in the devices that allow for these services and (just as importantly) have developed the new habits of utilizing such means of receiving goods and services, and many who lost jobs in traditional service and retail sectors have since found employment in online-related jobs. About two years following the start of the pandemic, inflation in the U.S. had soared to its highest levels since the 1980s for reasons that are debatable; yet, many economists suggest that the ease by which consumers were able to spend during the first two years of the pandemic—perhaps fueled by federal stimulus money—may have significantly contributed to this concerning economic development (Smialek, & Swanson, 2022).

Perhaps not surprisingly, given the contours of the pandemic, some business sectors have flourished while others have faltered. Given both the reality of increasing work-from-home and online work possibilities coupled with concerns of contracting the virus, the American hotel industry was projected to shrink by 45% in 2020 (Pandey, 2020). Similarly, movie theater attendance dramatically declined, with about half of pre-pandemic moviegoers who have not bought a ticket since (and may never do so again); in addition to concerns about the virus, with increased availability of viewing films online at significantly lower costs than visiting a theater, the entire traditional experience of going to a theater may need to be reconsidered (B. Barnes, 2021).

Even if Wall Street has fared much better than Main Street in the first several months following the pandemic (Choe et al., 2020), finance professor Noah Smith (2020) argued that the disastrous American response to the pandemic has had real economic costs for Americans juxtaposed with many other wealthy nations that had generally found more effective means and strategies for curtailing some of the more dire effects on its respective citizens which he termed "a painful and stark demonstration of national decline" (p. 4). Perhaps more ominously, he added:

> But the consequences of U.S. decline will far outlast coronavirus. With its high housing costs, poor infrastructure and transit, endemic gun violence, police brutality and bitter political and racial divisions, the U.S. will be a less appealing place for high-skilled workers to live. That means companies will find other countries in Europe, Asia and elsewhere a more attractive destination for investment, robbing the U.S. of jobs, depressing wages and draining away the local spending that powers the service economy. That in turn will exacerbate some of the worst trends of U.S. decline—less tax money means even more urban decay as infrastructure, education and social-welfare programs are forced to make big cuts...Almost every systematic economic advantage possessed by the U.S. is under threat. Unless there's a huge push to turn things around— to bring back immigrants, sustain research universities, make housing cheaper, lower infrastructure costs, reform the police and restore competence to the civil service—the result could be decades of stagnating or even declining living standards...if enough investors—foreign and domestic—lose confidence in the U.S.'s general effectiveness as a country...[America's financial] advantage will vanish. If capital begins to abandon the U.S....currency will crash...interest rates will be raised...and the country might undergo a period of stagflation worse than the 1970s. Large-scale unrest would undoubtedly result and—in the worst-case scenario—the U.S. could collapse like Venezuela (Smith, 2020, pp. 3-4).

Anthropologist Wade Davis struck a similar chord in a popular analysis which questioned how America could still retain its superpower status given that its share of Covid deaths—about a quarter of the world's total—far surpassed its expected amount when accounting for its population on a per capita basis; his argument though emphasized that "...the root of this transformation and decline lies an ever-widening chasm between Americans who have and those who have little or nothing" (DeCambre, 2020, p. 3).

To briefly reflect on this chapter, let me offer two summative conclusions that (while perhaps sobering) should not have necessarily been surprising: (1) the pandemic unleashed a whirlwind of economic changes (both for individuals and society) and (2) these associated economic threats contributed to some of the antisocial behavior displayed during the pandemic. Regarding the latter point, economic threat has often been associated with insecurity and prejudice in many contexts (Billiet et al., 2014); it is also a clear extension of realistic group conflict theory, which holds that intergroup hostility often occurs over competition for limited resources (e.g., Jackson, 1993). In reflecting on these trends though, it seems helpful to at least offer a reminder (as first noted in Chapter 1) that we cannot necessarily presume that the pandemic alone has produced the effects described in this chapter—whether they be, for instance, in terms of why so many workers have become discontent in their jobs or why many often aggressively pushed back against viral mitigation strategies. Even so, many of the trends and behaviors described in this chapter have at least been shaped by the pandemic and will likely continue to have significant consequences for our lives (individually and collectively) into the future.

References

Associated Press. (2021, July 27). No mask mandate, but Pennsylvania urged to follow guidance. *Associated Press.* https://apnews.com/article/government-and-politics-health-pennsylvania-coronavirus-pandemic-2ae32eedf62f143 d9653f305511b7278

Atterbury, A., & Perez, J., Jr. (2021, October 27). 'Threats of violence': School boards curb public comments to calm raucous meetings. *Politico.* https://www.politico.com/news/2021/10/27/school-boards-covid-restrictions-violence-517326

Balz, D., Clement, S., & Guskin, E. (2022, January 1). Republicans and Democrats divided over Jan. 6 insurrection and Trump's culpability, Post-UMD poll finds. *The Washington Post.* https://www.washingtonpost.com/politics/2022/01/01/post-poll-january-6/

Barnes, B. (2021, November 29). Movie theaters must 'urgently' rethink the experience, a study says. *The New York Times.* https://www.nytimes.com/2021/11/29/business/movie-theater-attendance.html

Barnes, R. (2021, December 20). Biden administration's vaccine requirements take center stage at Supreme Court. *The Washington Post.* https://www.washingtonpost.com/politics/courts_law/vaccine-mandate-supreme-court/2021/12/20/219651b8-61c1-11ec-8ce3-9454d0b46d42_story.html

Billiet, J., Meuleman, B., & De Witte, H. (2014). The relationship between ethnic threat and economic insecurity in times of economic crisis: Analysis of European Social Survey data. *Migration Studies, 2*(2), 135-161. https://doi.org/10.1093/migration/mnu023

Boone, R., Flaccus, G., & Kunzelman, M. (2021, January 13). Mix of extremists who stormed Capitol isn't retreating. *AP News.* https://apnews.com/article/capitol-siege-extremist-groups-80e309418abecd0b1d50ec4762e6d9c6

Brooks, K. J. (2020, June 9). Bracing for the next phase of the coronavirus recession: Bankruptcies. *CBS News.* https://www.cbsnews.com/news/bankruptcy-coronavirus-recession-2020/

Breuninger, K., & Kimball, S. (2022, January 13). Supreme Court blocks Biden Covid vaccine mandate for businesses, allows health-care worker rule. *CNBC.* https://www.cnbc.com/2022/01/13/supreme-court-ruling-biden-covid-vaccine-mandates.html

Choe, S., Veiga, A., & Rugaber, C. (2020, August 12). How can Wall Street be so healthy when Main Street isn't? *AP News.* https://apnews.com/article/virus-outbreak-financial-markets-ap-top-news-health-united-states-6cadd78335f d98926ffb1e5d6ecb2916

DeCambre, M. (2020, August 18/19). 'COVID has reduced to tatters the illusion of American exceptionalism,' anthropologist writes in Rolling Stone op-ed. *MarketWatch.* https://www.marketwatch.com/story/covid-has-reduced-to-tatters-the-illusion-of-american-exceptionalism-writes-rollingstone-in-op-ed-11597781594

Deliso, M. (2020, July 3). 'Unsafe': Women in public health facing pushback and threats for coronavirus response. *ABC News.* https://abcnews.go.com/Health/unsafe-women-public-health-facing-pushback-threats-coronavirus/story?id=71520262

Duncan, C. (2020, July 21). What did people say about wearing masks in the 1918 pandemic? It sounds familiar. *The Charlotte Observer.* https://www.charlotteobserver.com/news/coronavirus/article244267462.html

Ellerbeck, S. (2022, August 11). This country has the highest number of people planning to quit their jobs. *World Economic Forum.* https://www.weforum.org/agenda/2022/08/jobs-work-quit-great-resignation/

Feuer, J. (2020, June 29). CDC says U.S. has 'way too much virus' to control pandemic as cases surge across country. *CNBC.* https://www.cnbc.com/2020/06/29/cdc-says-us-has-way-too-much-virus-to-control-pandemic-as-cases-surge-across-country.html

Fisher, M. (2021, February 15). Eroding trust, spreading fear: The historical ties between pandemics and extremism. *The Washington Post.* https://www.washingtonpost.com/politics/pandemics-spawn-extremism/2021/02/14/d 4f7195c-6b1f-11eb-ba56-d7e2c8defa31_story.html

Forslid, R., & Herzing, M. (2021). Assessing the consequences of quarantines during a pandemic. *The European Journal of Health Economics, 22*(7), 1115-1128. https://doi.org/10.1007/s10198-021-01310-3

Gasparro, A., & Kang, J. (2020, July 12). From flour to canned soup, coronavirus surge pressures food supplies. *The Wall Street Journal.* https://www.wsj.com/articles/coronavirus-surge-challenges-struggling-food-supply-chains-11 594546200

Halverson, P. K., Yeager, V. A., Menachemi, N., Fraser, M. R., & Freeman, L. T. (2021). Public health officials and COVID-19: Leadership, politics, and the pandemic. *Journal of Public Health Management and Practice, 27*, S11-S13. https://doi.org/10.1097/PHH.0000000000001281

Hanna, M. (2021, October 31). Pennsbury's board president received threats of death and rape. She's not alone. *The Philadelphia Inquirer.* https://www.inquirer.com/news/school-board-threats-pennsylvania-20211031.html

Jackson, J. W. (1993). Realistic group conflict theory: A review and evaluation of the theoretical and empirical literature. *The Psychological Record, 43*(3), 395-414.

James, M. (2020, April 24). U.S. hits 50,000 deaths from coronavirus - just as many states announce plans to ease social restrictions. *USA Today.* https://www.usatoday.com/story/news/2020/04/24/coronavirus-united-states-death-us-hit-50-000-death-plateau-virus-friday/3017928001/

Jenkins, B. M. (2020, August 16). How the COVID-19 pandemic and George Floyd protests could give rise to terrorism. *NBC News.* https://www.nbcnews.com/think/opinion/how-covid-19-pandemic-george-floyd-protests-could-give-rise-ncna1236709

Kim, S. (2021, November 9). Who was Ryan White? Teen who contracted AIDS via blood transfusion. *Newsweek.* https://www.newsweek.com/ryan-white-teenager-aids-discrimination-hiv-history-1647301

King, M. (2021, October 28). First Covid raised the murder rate. Now it's changing the politics of crime. *Politico.* https://www.politico.com/news/2021/10/28/covid-murder-crime-rate-517226

Kounang, N. (2021, May 23). The pandemic has pushed more than 250 public health officials out the door. *CNN.* https://www.cnn.com/2021/05/23/health/public-health-officials-quit/index.html

Kretchmar, K., & Brewer, T. J. (2022). Neoliberalism, COVID, anti-science, and the politics of school reopening. *Education Policy Analysis Archives, 30,* (42). https://doi.org/10.14507/epaa.30.6959

Kurtz, H. (2021, November 11). Just how widespread are the threats to educators over COVID policies? *EducationWeek.* https://www.edweek.org/leadership/just-how-widespread-are-the-threats-to-educators-over-covid-policies/2021/11

Li, Y., Cheng, Z., Cai, X., Mao, Y., & Temkin-Greener, H. (2022). State social distancing restrictions and nursing home outcomes. *Scientific Reports, 12*(1), 1-11. https://doi.org/ 10.1038/s41598-022-05011-6

Lowrey, A. (2020, June 23). The second great depression. *The Atlantic.* https://www.theatlantic.com/ideas/archive/2020/06/second-great-depression/613360/

Mead, W. R. (2020, August 3). The pandemic is a dress rehearsal. *The Wall Street Journal.* https://www.wsj.com/articles/the-pandemic-is-a-dress-rehearsal-11596495140

Mello, M. M., Greene, J. A., & Sharfstein, J. M. (2020). Attacks on public health officials during COVID-19. *JAMA, 324*(8), 741-742. https://doi.org/10.1001/jama.2020.14423

Mims, C. (2020, November 2021). Four reasons the stay-at-home economy is here to stay. *The Wall Street Journal.* https://www.wsj.com/articles/four-reasons-the-stay-at-home-economy-is-here-to-stay-11605934806

Nicola, M., Alsafi, Z., Sohrabi, C., Kerwan, A., Al-Jabir, A., Iosifidis, C., Agha, M., & Agha, R. (2020). The socio-economic implications of the coronavirus pandemic (COVID-19): A review. *International Journal of Surgery, 78,* 185-193. https://doi.org/10.1016/j.ijsu.2020.04.018

Pandey, E. (2020, September 4). Hotel crisis hits new milestone. *Axios.* https://www.axios.com/hotel-crisis-coronavirus-economy-travel-556b1f8d-9a12-4555-8a94-a790d78f9bd3.html

Parker, K., & Horowitz, J. M. (2022, March 9). Majority of workers who quit a job in 2021 cite low pay, no opportunities for advancement, feeling disrespected. *Pew Research Center.* https://www.pewresearch.org/fact-tank/2022/03/09/majority-of-workers-who-quit-a-job-in-2021-cite-low-pay-no-opportunities-for-advancement-feeling-disrespected/

Rabinowitz, H. (2022, September 24). Judge dismisses lawsuit over DOJ memo on school board threats. *CNN.* https://www.cnn.com/2022/09/24/politics/doj-memo-school-board-threats-dismiss-lawsuit/index.html

Rose, J., & Baker, L. (2022, January 3). 6 in 10 Americans say U.S. democracy is in crisis as the 'Big Lie' takes root. *NPR.* https://www.npr.org/2022/01/03/1069764164/american-democracy-poll-jan-6

Sawchuk, S. (2021, July 29). Why school boards are now hot spots for nasty politics. *EducationWeek.* https://www.edweek.org/leadership/why-school-boards-are-now-hot-spots-for-nasty-politics/2021/07

Simmons-Duffin, S. (2021, December 16). As Omicron spreads, health experts push for mask mandates. But few states have one. *NPR.* https://www.npr.org/sections/health-shots/2021/12/16/1064668750/state-mask-mandates-omicron

Smialek, J., & Swanson, A. (2022, January 22). Rapid inflation fuels debate over what's to blame: Pandemic or policy. *The New York Times.* https://www.nytimes.com/2022/01/22/business/economy/inflation-biden-pandemic.html

Smith, N. (2020, June 29). Coronavirus brings American decline out in the open. *Bloomberg.* https://www.bloomberg.com/opinion/articles/2020-06-29/coronavirus-brings-american-decline-out-in-the-open

Strassmann, M. (2021, October 22). A record amount of Americans are quitting their jobs due to pandemic burnout. *CBS News.* https://www.cbsnews.com/news/covid-pandemic-burnout-americans-quit-jobs/

Thompson, D. (2021, October 7). America is running out of everything. *The Atlantic.* https://www.theatlantic.com/ideas/archive/2021/10/america-is-choking-under-an-everything-shortage/620322/

Topazian, R. J., McGinty, E. E., Han, H., Levine, A. S., Anderson, K. E., Presskreischer, R., & Barry, C. L. (2022). US adults' beliefs about harassing or threatening public health officials during the COVID-19 pandemic. *JAMA Network Open, 5*(7), e2223491-e2223491. https://doi.org/10.1001/jamanetworkopen.2022.23491

Tucker, E. (2021, April 8). Grim view of global future offered in intelligence report. *AP News.* https://apnews.com/article/technology-environment-us-news-coronavirus-pandemic-health-cbcafe70b4724a7605d56d40fa294027

Van Bavel, J. J., Baicker, K., Boggio, P. S., Capraro, V., Cichocka, A., Cikara, M., Crockett, M. J., Crum, A. J., Douglas, K. M., Druckman, J. N., Drury, J., Dube, O., Ellemers, N., Finkel, E. J., Fowler, J. H., Gelfand, M., Han, S., Haslam, S. A., Jetten, J., ... & Willer, R. (2020). Using social and behavioural science to support COVID-19 pandemic response. *Nature Human Behaviour, 4*(5), 460-471. https://doi.org/10.1038/s41562-020-0884-z

Van Kessel, P., & Silver, L. (2021, November 18). Where Americans find meaning in life has changed over the past four years. *Pew Research Center.* https://www.pewresearch.org/fact-tank/2021/11/18/where-americans-find-meaning-in-life-has-changed-over-the-past-four-years/

Vasel, K. (2021, October 8). These people quit their jobs during the pandemic. Here's what they're doing now. *CNN*. https://www.cnn.com/2021/10/08/success/quit-job-pandemic-feseries/index.html

Wall Street Journal. (2020, June 27). Six months that shook the world. *The Wall Street Journal*. https://www.wsj.com/articles/six-months-that-shook-the-world-11593231014

Ward, J. A., Stone, E. M., Mui, P., & Resnick, B. (2022). Pandemic-related workplace violence and its impact on public health officials, March 2020–January 2021. *American Journal of Public Health, 112*(5), 736-746. https://doi.org/10.2105/AJPH.2021.306649

Woodward, B., & Costa, R. (2021). *Peril*. Simon & Schuster.

Wu, K. J. (2021, July 22). 4 reasons I'm wearing a mask again. *The Atlantic*. https://www.theatlantic.com/health/archive/2021/07/fully-vaccinated-masking-delta/619532/

CHAPTER FOUR

Personal and Interpersonal Challenges

This chapter highlights some of the key personal and interpersonal challenges emanating from the pandemic. Using both early research and news analyses, this chapter attempts to portray a psychological portrait of many of the common difficulties faced by both individuals and couples or families, including (but not limited to) concerns of social distancing, fear, loneliness, and domestic violence.

Personal Challenges: Disrupted and Interrupted Lives

From the earliest weeks of the pandemic, it was widely commented that a general sense of unease about this "new normal" was quite common as it upended our routines and heightened many broad ranging fears and anxieties (Rubinstein, 2020) that were also laced with an innate sense of grief that life would just somehow be now different (Berinato, 2020). Coelho et al. (2020) suggest, among other factors, that tolerance of the unknown and social isolation as well as lower general anxiety may have been beneficial in coping with the uncertainties generated by the pandemic. Indeed, young adults with pre-existing anxiety were particularly apt to report greater stressors during the pandemic (Morales et al., 2022). Perhaps not surprisingly, individual difference variables like resilience, higher subjective happiness and life satisfaction, and strategies for adapting to adversity tended to be most associated with greater adaptation to the stresses of the pandemic, whereas higher neuroticism and lower extraversion were not (Morales-Vives et al., 2020). Cheng et al. (2021) noted that four major forms of Covid related anxiety involved anxiety over personal health, societal health, others' reactions, and economic problems—and yet, coping flexibility was largely inversely associated with these worries by being able to utilize coping strategies to meet specific situational demands which helped to promote adaptation. Despite these unique and vast challenges that the Covid pandemic represented, perhaps we can take comfort in knowing that the ways and means of dealing with these challenges largely mimic many of the well-known processes individuals have previously used when confronting other serious life events and difficulties.

The aforesaid points notwithstanding, in March 2021, the American Psychological Association (2021) released a comprehensive report detailing the profound challenges impacting the American population at large. Of particular note, about half of all participants reported greater stress in their lives since the start of the pandemic and majorities (or near majorities) reported adverse impacts regarding their weight, sleeping habits, or attention to their health care; African-Americans and younger adults (i.e., Generation Z) were particularly apt to voice concerns over their future or general mental health. It was also notable that 82% of this sample never expected the pandemic to last for as long as it has persisted. In reflecting on the one-year anniversary of the start of the pandemic in America (when then-President Trump declared a national emergency following the World Health Organization's declaration of a pandemic) in March 2021, psychologist John Duffy (2021) aptly summed up the disruption and downright despair many have felt:

> We've lost so much in this year of devastation, so many of the normal markers of life we typically take for granted. We missed graduations, holidays, sports seasons, plays, weddings, funerals, huggings, spontaneity and just connecting face to face with friends and family. Many of us have lost people we love. Meanwhile, negativity and judgment run high, with most every issue being polarized, down to the wearing of masks. As a result, people feel disconnected and isolated. More of my clients report experiencing a higher sense of self-doubt than ever before. Many of us feel a degree of hopelessness and despair we could not have imagined a year ago (pp. 1-2).

Arguably, most Americans were not prepared (physically or mentally) to realize how the pandemic would become such a pervasive event. Perhaps this view was reinforced by media reports such as one from June 30, 2020, stating: "Just as a lot of us were beginning to maybe put Coronavirus in the rear-view mirror, this past week and a half has shown that it's not over yet" (Havener, 2020, p. 1). Around the same time as the aforesaid media report, Loofbourow (2020) wondered in amazement as to how so many Americans would just shirk off the virus as if they themselves could do so (as opposed to the reality that viruses are immune to public opinion); she considered an array of factors from American individualism, Trump's nonresponsiveness, and America's increasing normalization of death (e.g., the relative common reality of mass casualty events). But, ultimately, her analysis may boil down to a psychological truth that has been borne out many times in the research literature:

> Constant alarm is unsustainable, and we've gotten used to crises rapid-cycling so that we drop and forget one kind of alarm in order to pick up another...The muscles we use to panic with are ready to move on. The problem is, the virus isn't (Loofbourow, 2020, p. 6).

The pandemic has left many Americans with both a literal and realistic sense that time has somehow been lost or evaded them whether it be the "Groundhog Day" (in reference to the 1993 comedy film) sense of constantly repeating one's day over and over (and, in the process feeling less focused and more lethargic; e,g., Kohler, 2021) or by losing one's prior routine to more consequential realities of lost time spent with loved ones, deferred medical treatments, or other professional or personal plans (Arkin et al., 2020). The lack of distinctiveness, in part, has given many the sense that the first two years of the pandemic have been one big blur—and, there is evidence that both prospective and working memory have declined during the pandemic (Judkis, 2022). Moreover, staying home during the pandemic was commonly viewed as a form of confinement and often linked to feelings of depression and helplessness (Bozdağ, 2021). Relatedly, close adherence to social distancing guidelines was associated with several declines in psychological well-being that were not even remedied with the presence of technology-based communication (Ford, 2021).

In September 2020, former Assistant Secretary for Homeland Security and professor at Harvard's Kennedy School of Government Juliette Kayyem (2020) suggested that an inherent problem that many have faced was a common feeling of impatience in terms of when the pandemic would be "over;" however, another part of this problem, as she suggested, is that "[w]e've been psychologically kicking the can down the road" (p. 3). This crisis may have felt akin to Lucy removing the football from Charlie Brown any time he got about to kick it. In other words, in the first few months of the pandemic, there was a potential hope that Covid might follow a flu-like pattern and not be present in the summer. It didn't follow that plan. Then, there was a hope that with a new presidential administration headed by Joe Biden that the release of vaccines would help us find the end. But, it didn't entirely—as discussed elsewhere in this book, there were new variants, select blunders from the Biden administration, and significant amounts of vaccine hesitancy or refusal. To the degree that individuals may have simply wished for a quick "end" to this crisis, it can indeed reflect a sense of impatience—or the discomforting reality that life will never quite be the same as before Covid (Walsh, 2020). Likewise, that leaders did not fully understand or address to the broader public the challenges to a return of a new normalcy, this underscores the importance of such frank directives. Life is replete with personal and collective choices. We can choose to not mask or vaccinate, but that has implications for our own and the larger public health. Governments can choose to act and that too has consequences. For instance, the world would now likely be a very different place if the United States decided to remain neutral during World War II. In that respect, competent leaders need to consider the consequences of their actions (or inactions) and disseminate that to the larger public as well.

Of course, though, each of us are ultimately responsible for our own mental health—and it has been indeed tested during this prolonged stressor. Gobbi and colleagues (2020) offer evidence that has been consistent with much prior research that those with previous psychological problems or psychiatric conditions may have faced some of the most profound challenges in coping with the pandemic.

Interpersonal and Family Challenges

It is difficult to fully quantify the myriad of ways and examples that both individual and family lives have been challenged and disrupted due to the pandemic. The challenges that couples have faced due to the pandemic have, at some level, been both surprising yet not altogether unexpected. In the early months of the pandemic, both marriage and divorce rates had decreased over the previous year—though much of this decline may be attributed to the practical realities of not being able to go through these procedures (e.g., due to shutdowns), financial implications, or concern about making dramatic life changes during a pandemic and the related threats. The reality of spending one's time in (or near) constant contact with one's partner while managing other daily life challenges (such as other work, household, or child-care commitments) while likely having to significantly modify one's pre-pandemic daily routine created stressful conditions even for couples whose relationships were not troubled prior to the pandemic (Crary, 2021). But, the decline in divorce rate had been occurring prior to the pandemic—and, on a positive note, there is evidence that over half of all married Americans felt that the pandemic made them appreciate their spouse more and there was a deeper commitment to their marriage (Wang, 2020). Exactly how couples may have fared in the pandemic may have largely been a function of pandemic-related stressors along with personal vulnerabilities (including the pre-pandemic health of the relationship; Pietromonaco & Overall, 2022).

Given the profound social disruption created due to the pandemic (e.g., confinement, job losses) and strains on caregiving, this created the potential for much stress for all individual members and the family as a whole; however, the pandemic did not inherently have to create deep strains provided that families could harness resilience (e.g., through communication and fostering broader family beliefs) of the family unit (Prime et al., 2020). Benoit (2021) discusses the potentially double-edged phenomenon of how many couples have been in near constant contact with each since the pandemic (which can be associated with its own share of stresses) and, because of this shift, may be feeling a sense of post-pandemic separation anxiety. Though divorce (and marriage) rates declined in 2020, as previously noted, it is not necessarily because couples grew closer but rather due to logistical and financial practicalities related to the pandemic (Steverman, 2021). To that point, an online survey of over 1500 adults (Lehmiller et al., 2021), found that half of all participants showed declines in their sexual lives. However, perhaps being fueled by feelings of loneliness and stress, about twenty percent of their sample (particularly amongst younger adults) were more open to exploring more novel sexual practices.

On an encouraging note, Holmberg et al. (2022) found that in the early months of the pandemic, couples (residing in the United States) were more likely to focus on positive rather than negative themes such as appreciating the relationship and taking advantage of the increased time together. Yet, one of the one of the most troubling consequences of the pandemic has been the moderate to strong increases in domestic violence following lockdown periods particularly with respect to U.S. population data (Piquero et al., 2021). However, some subsequent analyses of crime reports from 18 major U.S. police departments failed to support claims that the shutdowns caused increased domestic violence; though there were increases for domestic calls at the start of the pandemic they preceded mandatory shutdowns and there were declines once the shutdowns were implemented (Miller et al., 2022). Another disturbing phenomenon during the pandemic involved reports of children or adolescents showing acts of abuse or violence towards their parents; one report from the United Kingdom covering their April-June 2020 Covid lockdown suggested reported increases from both parents and practitioners of upwards of 70% increases of violent episodes that may have been fomented by confinement, changes in routine, fear and anxiety, and insufficient social support (Condry et al., 2020). Even if there remains some debates over the prevalence of reported episodes of abuse, Wake and Kandula (2022) contend that the pandemic has augmented domestic violence vulnerabilities against women and children worldwide due, in part, to the (often interconnected) stresses of the pandemic, financial insecurities, and addiction.

To highlight a case that shows how two different family dynamics that were altered due to the pandemic, consider parents who expected their child to have left for college in 2020 and, in doing so, expected to experience a so-called "empty nest" (Donnelly, 2020). The pandemic shook up the very notion of an empty nest as many adult children returned to live with their elderly parents (Kurutz, 2021); in fact, a Pew Research Center report found that 52% of young adults (between the ages of 18-29) had been living with at least one parent in July 2020—which was higher than the last measured value from available Census data in 1940 from the Great Depression era (Shoichet, 2020). Understandably, many college students (particularly freshmen) who were looking forward to a traditional college experience in the Fall 2020 semester may have been disappointed or vastly changed their plans (Fox, 2020; Tanner, 2020); likewise, parents may have been faced with a mix of emotions about concern for their adult children's physical and emotional wellbeing but also their own sense of trying to comprehend how their personal feelings and familial relations were changing (Thompson, 2020). The graduating class of 2020 (and the larger Generation Z cohort) found themselves dealing not with just a national crisis but a moment that may have lasting effects as they traverse through emerging adulthood years and beyond (e.g., Volpe, 2022). Not only was the Class of 2020 largely unable to enjoy traditional graduation ceremonies, but they also lost the solace of physical contact with their peers and the school (or college) environment, along with entering a period of great uncertainty for their lives and future educational and vocational pursuits (Alter, 2020).

Loneliness and Loss of Social Connections

In many respects, the pandemic has trained us to at least be scared or wary of others, given the fact that anyone could have been potentially carrying and transmitting the virus to us without our knowledge (Miller, 2020). To some degree, it may take some time to feel comfortable interacting with others again, particularly in larger group settings (Ward, 2021). Individual differences are also important to consider in terms of how loneliness is perceived and experienced. For instance, though introverts may have missed opportunities to spend time with close others during the pandemic, such social disruptions may have been less problematic than for extraverts who prefer and tend to actively seek out social connections with others (Roberts, 2021). There is also the concern that those who may opt to wear masks indefinitely may be doing so at the cost of missing out on possible social connections and perhaps even doing so to mask social anxiety (Peyser, 2021). Saint and Moscovitch (2021) add that further research is needed regarding the possible links between social anxiety and mask-wearing but suggest that, as mask-wearing becomes less commonplace, this may be particularly distressing for those with social anxiety due to increases in uncertainty and fear about whether their choices are being judged by others.

On a more hopeful note, even if adults may have had concerns about the well-being of loved ones or themselves and fears about being able to achieve their goals, the pandemic may have provided people with an opportunity to renew their sense of gratitude for family and friends (Melore, 2020). In a similar vein, those who have suffered with chronic illness may have felt that the pandemic gave others an appreciation for what it feels like to be more limited in one's daily activities—and there may be some lamenting the fact that this new-found appreciation may wane as the pandemic's more dire effects potentially decrease (Grunwald, 2021). And, people still have found potentially new and innovative ways to connect with others particularly in an online fashion. For instance, men's friendships have historically placed a particularly valued premium on activities, such as sports; with closures or more limited opportunities to congregate, many men may have had to find new ways of communicating with each other aided with the help of technology that they may not have necessarily been as accustomed to prior to the pandemic (Schmidt, 2020).

Some of the earliest research on the state of loneliness from the first two years of the pandemic suggests there has not necessarily been a radically altered shift in terms of how loneliness is experienced and who precisely is more likely to feel lonely. Consistent with pre- Covid research, reported loneliness during the pandemic was a significant risk factor for depression and anxiety (Palgi et al., 2020). In the initial pandemic lockdowns, as is often reported in the literature, women and those living alone tended to report greater feelings of loneliness—though younger people (including students) and those with lower incomes had greater loneliness than usual (Bu et al., 2020). In a review of over 50 studies examining social isolation and loneliness in the earliest stages of the pandemic, Buecker and Horstmann (2022) found that perceptions of loneliness remained fairly stable post-Covid; however, there was a reported decline in the quality of social relationships and the number of social interactions experienced as the pandemic progressed.

In reflecting on many of these early trends and experiences regarding personal and interpersonal challenges of the pandemic, it is important to put these trends in some context. In the two years following its onset, most of the behavioral phenomena that defined much of the pandemic's earliest phases and realities—lockdowns, social distancing, face masks, and lack of vaccine availability—have all largely (though not necessarily entirely) become relics from that time period. While additional research might help to further flesh out some of the trends detailed in this chapter, perhaps an even greater future question will be how the challenges individuals faced during the pandemic have impacted them in the long-term.

References

Alter, C. (2020, May 21). How COVID-19 will shape the Class of 2020 for the rest of their lives. *Time.* https://time.com/5839765/college-graduation-2020/

American Psychological Association. (2021, March). Stress in America: One year later, a new wave of pandemic health concerns. *American Psychological Association.* https://www.apa.org/news/press/releases/stress/2021/sia-pandemic-report.pdf

Arkin, D., Fichtel, C., & Walters. (2020, December 29). The lost year: How Covid-19 left many Americans 'stuck in time.' *NBC News.* https://www.nbcnews.com/news/us-news/lost-year-how-covid-19-left-many-americans-stuck-time-n1252152

Benoit, S. (2021, March 31). Are you dealing with post-pandemic separation anxiety? *GQ.* https://www.gq.com/story/post-pandemic-separation-anxiety

Berinato, S. (2020, March 23). That discomfort you're feeling is grief. *Harvard Business Review.* https://hbr.org/2020/03/that-discomfort-youre-feeling-is-grief

Bozdağ, F. (2021). The psychological effects of staying home due to the COVID-19 pandemic. *The Journal of General Psychology, 148*(3), 226-248. https://doi.org/10.1080/00221309.2020.1867494

Bu, F., Steptoe, A., & Fancourt, D. (2020). Who is lonely in lockdown? Cross-cohort analyses of predictors of loneliness before and during the COVID-19 pandemic. *Public Health, 186,* 31-34. https://doi.org/10.1016/j.socscimed.2020.113521

Buecker, S., & Horstmann, K. T. (2021). Loneliness and social isolation during the COVID-19 pandemic: A systematic review enriched with empirical evidence from a large-scale diary study. *European Psychologist, 26*(4), 272. http://dx.doi.org/10.1027/1016-9040/a000453

Cheng, C., Wang, H. Y., & Ebrahimi, O. V. (2021). Adjustment to a "new normal:" Coping flexibility and mental health issues during the COVID-19 pandemic. *Frontiers in Psychiatry, 12,* 626197. https://doi.org/10.3389/fpsyt.2021.626197

Coelho, C. M., Suttiwan, P., Arato, N., & Zsido, A. N. (2020). On the nature of fear and anxiety triggered by COVID-19. *Frontiers in Psychology, 11,* 581314. https://doi.org/10.3389/fpsyg.2020.581314

Condry, R., Miles, C., Brunton-Douglas, T., & Oladapo, A. (2020) Experiences of child and adolescent to parent violence in the Covid-19 Pandemic. *University of Oxford.* https://www.law.ox.ac.uk/sites/files/oxlaw/final_report_capv_in_covid-19_aug20.pdf

Crary, D. (2021, February 14). Marriage and divorce amid pandemic: Couples' challenges abound. *AP News.* https://apnews.com/article/marriage-divorce-amid-coronavirus-c004c459d5007ec9f57297906c270787

Donnelly, E. (2020, August 26). Empty nest on hold: Parents share what it's like to have their college freshmen stay home. *Yahoo!Life.* https://www.yahoo.com/lifestyle/empty-nest-on-hold-pandemic-162248107.html

Duffy, J. (2021, March 13). A year into the pandemic, it's time to take stock of our mental health. *CNN.* https://www.cnn.com/2021/03/11/health/take-stock-mental-health-covid-pandemic-wellness/index.html

Ford, M. B. (2021). Social distancing during the COVID-19 pandemic as a predictor of daily psychological, social, and health-related outcomes. *The Journal of General Psychology, 148*(3), 249-271. https://doi.org/10.1080/00221309.2020.1860890

Fox, M. (2020, June 17). Half of recent high school grads have changed their plans due to coronavirus. *CNBC.* https://www.cnbc.com/2020/06/17/49percent-of-recent-high-school-grads-have-changed-plans-due-to-covid-19.html

Gobbi, S., Płomecka, M.B., Ashraf, Z, Radziński, P., Neckels, R., Lazzeri, S., Dedić, A., Bakalović, A., Hrustić, L., Skórko, B., Haghi, S. E., Almazidou, K., Rodríguez-Pino, L., Alp, A.B., Jabeen, H., Waller, V., Shibli, D., Behnam, M.A., Arshad, A.H., ... & Jawaid, A. (2020). Worsening of preexisting psychiatric conditions during the COVID-19 pandemic. *Frontiers in Psychiatry, 11,* 5814261407. https://doi.org/10.3389/fpsyt.2020.581426

Grunwald, L. (2021, April 9). I worry I'll be left behind when the pandemic ends. *The Atlantic.* https://www.theatlantic.com/ideas/archive/2021/04/when-pandemic-ends-i-worry-ill-be-left-behind/618547/

Havener, C. (2020, June 30). How reopening, young people, and protesters are playing into PA's Coronavirus uptick. *WJAC.* https://wjactv.com/news/coronavirus/how-reopening-young-people-and-protesters-are-playing-into-pas-coronavirus-uptick

Holmberg, D., Bell, K. M., & Cadman, K. (2022). Now for the good news: Self-perceived positive effects of the first pandemic wave on romantic relationships outweigh the negative. *Journal of Social and Personal Relationships, 39*(1), 34-55. https://doi.org/10.1177/02654075211050939

Judkis, M. (2022, January 20). Greetings from the pandemic memory hole, where the last two years are one big blur. *The Washington Post.* https://www.washingtonpost.com/lifestyle/2022/01/20/pandemic-memory-covid-2020-2021-2022/

Kayyem, J. (2020, September 6). The emotionally challenging next phase of the pandemic. *The Atlantic.* https://www.theatlantic.com/ideas/archive/2020/09/americas-coronavirus-ordeal-wont-end-when-2020-does/616108/

Kohler, L. (2021, January 27). How to break the Covid-19 Groundhog Day cycle. *Forbes.* https://www.forbes.com/sites/lindsaykohler/2021/01/27/how-to-break-the-covid-19-groundhog-day-cycle

Kurutz, S. (2021, February 5). Getting to know you, again. *The New York Times.* https://www.nytimes.com/2021/02/05/realestate/moving-in-with-your-parents.html

Lehmiller, J. J., Garcia, J. R., Gesselman, A. N., & Mark, K. P. (2021). Less sex, but more sexual diversity: Changes in sexual behavior during the COVID-19 coronavirus pandemic. *Leisure Sciences, 43*(1-2), 295-304. https://doi.org/10.1080/01490400.2020.1774016

Loofbourow, L. (2020, June 26). Americans are sick of the pandemic. The pandemic is not sick of us. *Slate.* https://slate.com/news-and-politics/2020/06/americas-pandemic-not-over-yet.html

Melore, C. (2020, August 25). COVID-19 leaves bucket lists in limbo: 7 in 10 fear poor health will cut memorable life experiences short. *Study Finds.* https://www.studyfinds.org/coronavirus-bucket-list-poor-health-life-experiences/

Miller, A. R., Segal, C., & Spencer, M. K. (2022). Effects of COVID-19 shutdowns on domestic violence in US cities. *Journal of Urban Economics, 131*, 103476. https://doi.org/10.1016/j.jue.2022.103476

Miller, E. D. (2020). Loneliness in the era of COVID-19. *Frontiers in Psychology, 11*, 2219. https://doi.org/10.3389/fpsyg.2020.02219

Morales, S., Zeytinoglu, S., Lorenzo, N. E., Chronis-Tuscano, A., Degnan, K. A., Almas, A. N., Pine, D. S., & Fox, N. A. (2022). Which anxious adolescents were most affected by the COVID-19 pandemic? *Clinical Psychological Science.* https://doi.org/10.1177/21677026211059524

Morales-Vives, F., Dueñas, J. M., Vigil-Colet, A., & Camarero-Figuerola, M. (2020). Psychological variables related to adaptation to the COVID-19 lockdown in Spain. *Frontiers in Psychology, 11*, 565634. https://doi.org/10.3389/fpsyg.2020.565634

Palgi, Y., Shrira, A., Ring, L., Bodner, E., Avidor, S., Bergman, Y., Cohen-Fridel, S, Keisari, S., & Hoffman, Y. (2020). The loneliness pandemic: Loneliness and other concomitants of depression, anxiety and their comorbidity during the COVID-19 outbreak. *Journal of Affective Disorders, 275*, 109. http://doi.org/10.1016/j.jad.2020.06.036

Peyser, E. (2021, April 19). The forever maskers. *Intelligencer.* https://nymag.com/intelligencer/2021/04/the-people-who-plan-on-wearing-masks-forever.html#comments

Pietromonaco, P. R., & Overall, N. C. (2022). Implications of social isolation, separation, and loss during the COVID-19 pandemic for couples' relationships. *Current Opinion in Psychology, 43*, 189-194. https://doi.org/10.1016/j.copsyc.2021.07.014

Piquero, A. R., Jennings, W. G., Jemison, E., Kaukinen, C., & Knaul, F. M. (2021). Domestic violence during the COVID-19 pandemic-Evidence from a systematic review and meta-analysis. *Journal of Criminal Justice, 74*, 101806. https://doi.org/10.1016/j.jcrimjus.2021.101806

Prime, H., Wade, M., & Browne, D. T. (2020). Risk and resilience in family well-being during the COVID-19 pandemic. *American Psychologist, 75* (5), 631-643. http://dx.doi.org/10.1037/amp0000660

Roberts, R. (2021, April 10). Meet the introverts who are dreading a return to normal. *The Washington Post.* https://www.washingtonpost.com/lifestyle/style/introverts-are-dreading-a-return-to-the-noise-crowds-and-small-talk-of-normal-life/2021/04/09/386006b0-987b-11eb-b28d-bfa7bb5cb2a5_story.html

Rubinstein, P. (2020, May 27). Why do we feel uneasy about a 'new normal'? *BBC.* https://www.bbc.com/worklife/article/20200521-why-do-we-feel-uneasy-about-a-new-normal

Saint, S. A., & Moscovitch, D. A. (2021). Effects of mask-wearing on social anxiety: An exploratory review. *Anxiety, Stress, & Coping, 34*(5), 487-502. https://doi.org/10.1080/10615806.2021.1929936

Schmidt, S. (2020, November 30). No game days. No bars. The pandemic is forcing some men to realize they need deeper friendships. *The Washington Post.* https://www.washingtonpost.com/road-to-recovery/2020/11/30/male-bonding-covid/

Shoichet, C. E. (2020, September 4). 52% of young adults in the US are living with their parents. That's the highest share since the Great Depression. *CNN.* https://www.cnn.com/2020/09/04/us/children-living-with-parents-pandemic-pew/index.html

Steverman, B. (2021, January 5). Divorces and marriages tumbled in U.S. during Covid, study shows. *Bloomberg.* https://www.bloombergquint.com/onweb/divorces-and-marriages-tumbled-in-u-s-during-covid-study-shows

Tanner, L. (2020, October 24). Stressed freshmen missing quintessential college experience. *AP News.* https://apnews.com/article/race-and-ethnicity-virus-outbreak-anxiety-health-f51199511ef1a31540b5ecaaf28805ea

Thompson, K. (2020, June). Empty nest during a pandemic: Facing your fear and grief in 2020. *Smart College Visit.* https://smartcollegevisit.com/2020/06/empty-nest-during-pandemic-fear-grief.html

Volpe, J. D. (2022). *Fight: How Gen Z is channeling their fear and passion to save America*. St. Martin's Press.

Wake, A. D., & Kandula, U. R. (2022). The global prevalence and its associated factors toward domestic violence against women and children during COVID-19 pandemic—"The shadow pandemic": A review of cross-sectional studies. *Women's Health, 18.* https://doi.org/10.1177/17455057221095536

Walsh, N. P. (2020, September 30). There is no getting 'back to normal,' experts say. The sooner we accept that, the better. *CNN.* https://www.cnn.com/2020/09/30/health/back-to-normal-bias-wellness/index.html

Wang, W. (2020, November 10). The U.S. divorce rate has hit a 50-year low. *Institute for Family Studies.* https://ifstudies.org/blog/the-us-divorce-rate-has-hit-a-50-year-low

Ward, M. (2021, April 7). Not everyone is ready for the pandemic to end. *Politico.* https://www.politico.com/newsletters/politico-nightly/2021/04/02/not-everyone-is-ready-for-the-pandemic-to-end-492346

CHAPTER FIVE

Loss, Grief, and Mental Health Concerns

Threats to Mental Health

In many respects, this chapter is an extension of the previous one. But, it is subtly different in that it aims to provide a greater voice to the personal psychological toll the pandemic has taken on many—and, indeed, such documentation is critical to understanding personal pain and loss (Harvey, 2000). To wit, in an April 2021 TED talk, psychologist Dr. Rachel Wernicke asked the audience to consider what their "Covid story" would be and then adds: "many of them are heavy because that's the global story of Covid of suffering and of death and for too many people the story about the pandemic will be about their mental illness" (Wernicke, 2021, 1:00). She further adds that much of this trauma has unfolded in the context of both stigma of mental illness, a dubious mental health care treatment system, and particularly insidious challenges associated with anxiety and depression for younger adults. Consistent with the themes from her TED talk, the pandemic presented an overwhelming narrative of loss, grief, and larger mental health concerns. As such, this chapter aims to offer a deeper consideration of the many mental health crises wrought by the pandemic along with some context from the larger loss and trauma/ stress and coping literature.

Indeed, a plethora of prominent and respected organizations have clearly documented the toll that the pandemic has taken on Americans' mental health. In an odd coincidence, the start of the pandemic largely corresponded with the constitutionally mandated U.S. Census count. At the recommendation of the Centers for Disease Control and Prevention's National Center for Health Statistics, two brief common screening tools for depression (PHQ-2) and anxiety (GAD-2) were added to the Census Bureau's emergency coronavirus project, which indicated that about 24% and 30% of American adults showed significant clinical criteria for the presence of major depressive disorder and generalized anxiety disorder, respectively; these trends were particularly pronounced amongst women as well as younger and poorer adults (Fowers & Wan, 2020). Additional surveys conducted in 2020 by both the American Psychological Association and American Psychiatric Association confirmed the strains and mental health threats associated with the pandemic such that about 80% of American adults felt that the pandemic was a major source of stress in their lives (where two-thirds felt increased stress as the pandemic continued on) and 62% of Americans felt more anxious than the previous year (Carloss, 2020).

Though it has been steadily increasing ever since 2014, Gallup's Negative Experience Index revealed its highest level to date in 2020 when surveying adults in 115 countries; four in ten adults reported feeling worry or stress and nearly three in ten adults reported physical pain, sadness, or anger (Ray, 2021). In the earliest weeks of the pandemic, in April 2020, Park and colleagues (2020) found that adults were particularly concerned about the possible severity of the virus, how (and how long) to maintain appropriate preventative measures, and financial concerns.

Children were likewise vastly impacted by the initial realities of the pandemic. For instance, Bignardi and colleagues (2021) documented significant and medium-to-large effects of increased depression amongst 7-11-year-old children during the United Kingdom lockdown period of April to June 2020. Mental illness symptomology (e.g., for depression, anxiety, and substance abuse) have all increased since—and perhaps, at least to a degree, due to—the pandemic to upwards of about 41% of all respondents from a summer 2020 CDC survey (Thomas & Romano, 2020). Perhaps this should not be surprising following the major disruptive emergency that the pandemic represented. As concerning as that may be, the larger question is how pervasive or long-lasting these trends may be in the future (Demopoulos, 2020). Even so, it is critical to emphasize the great emotional toll that the pandemic has already had on the general public, essential workers, and Covid survivors with individuals contending with stressful and grief-related reactions that they may have never had to cope with previously; moreover, some of the disruptions to students' opportunities to socialize and learn in more traditional ways may also pose some developmental challenges (Seow, 2020).

Part of what has made the pandemic so disorienting for many is its association with a perpetual state of ambiguity; this, in turn, is often associated with higher potential anxiety in that we cannot always clearly know whether our chosen acts will be associated with potential rewards or punishments—which is, by contrast, what allows for making risk far less troubling to our minds (Sapolsky, 2020). Psychologist Adam Grant (2021) argued that our brains were largely charged with threat-detection in the early stages of the pandemic. He further argues that this acute feeling of anguish has largely (particularly in 2021) given way to one of languish marked by a lack of well-being; in essence, as the pandemic wore on, languishing did not necessarily suggest the presence of mental illness or depression but rather with decreased functioning and motivation. To the degree that individuals were focusing on negative or stressful effects of the pandemic coupled with a more static routine post-pandemic, this may have further contributed to a confused sense of time perception (Nemo, 2020). Part of the reason why such "brain fog" may have been experienced by others is due to memory, attentional, and processing impairments and difficulties due to not as much varied stimulation as a function of the lockdowns and related behavioral modifications associated with the pandemic (Sarner, 2021). A real-world concerning consequence of possible cognitive load associated with the mundane existence of pandemic life (such as hours spent doing work online or videoconferencing) could be an increase in motor vehicle accidents and death; but, this is yet another example of the importance of not necessarily drawing causal connections since there is also evidence that, with fewer Americans routinely driving, many are doing so recklessly and at increased speeds (Eisenstein, 2021).

With potentially increasing numbers of individuals more willing to seek therapy in the wake of the pandemic (Melore, 2021), psychologists had to quickly modify various facets and modalities of their practice (including online delivery) while simultaneously often confronting their own feelings of burnout (Shklarski et al., 2021). On a more optimistic note, clinical psychologists (among others) have been quick to remind us that we do not have to passively assume an existence fraught with bleakness or despair during the pandemic. In fact, Norcross and Phillips (2020) maintain that self-care is particularly critical with an emphasis on the following practical behavioral and mental strategies: limiting media coverage, maintaining a routine, cognitive restructuring (where we objectively question negative thoughts), practicing gratitude and mindfulness, connecting with others, safely engaging with nature, and showing self-empathy. Indeed, with the inherent uncertainty and upheaval associated with the pandemic, trying to stay focused on the current moment (e.g., through meditation and mindfulness)—instead of considering what the future may hold may be particularly important for our mental health and well-being (Brooks, 2020).

Loss and Grief

Prominent author Hope Edelman (2020) offered a very poignant Tweet on December 30, 2020, that described her pain in reflecting on 2020: "2020 gave me a #divorce, a pandemic, the near collapse of my company, an empty nest, and having to sell my home of 23 yrs—and how messed up is it that this makes me one of the #lucky ones because no one in my family died." Though the personal pain from her statement seems fairly evident, it is also telling that she at least found some solace in the fact that she did not have to contend with the death of any loved ones. Tragically, too many individuals did have to do so—and not being able to often attend funerals (particularly as was often the case in other notable calamities like 9/11 or the 1980s AIDS crisis) likely heightened this grief for many (Siemaszko, 2020). Graff (2021) argues that the loss and grief that is so palpable to many is not necessarily resonating with the American public at large due to the many political divisions detailed in this book. He further suggested that this is a particularly glaring contrast to the 9/11 terrorist attacks, where Americans largely came together (at least for a time) following that disaster and that point may have had an even greater poignancy given that the twentieth-anniversary commemoration took place during the pandemic. Regarding the contrast between the pandemic and 9/11, grief counselor David Kessler made a very apt point suggesting the inherent sense of disenfranchised grief that many who have lost loved ones to the pandemic may feel:

> But almost no one, after 9/11, told a relative of a victim, 'I don't know if that's true that he or she died in a terror attack...Here, a national crisis has been taken over by politics, and the very existence of the pandemic has been questioned. People have died, and we're still debating whether to wear masks (Siemaszko, 2020, p. 3).

On New Year's Day in 2021, psychotherapist F. Diane Barth (2021) offered an analysis reminding us that we can be resilient in the face of loss and trauma—and indeed, we can find meaning in it and even potentially finds bits of personally perceived positive moments and occurrences that took place in the year 2020. The pandemic though is a more uniquely qualitative event insomuch that it does not represent a singular happening, like a terrorist attack or death of a loved one. It has been an ongoing stressor that potentially can cause life-altering consequences like coping with a chronic disease—and, it is generally believed to be associated with more severe negative outcomes (Stroebe & Schut, 2021). Indeed, as a globally shared event that can produce stress, loss, and trauma, it is widely believed that complicated grief requiring psychological or psychiatric treatment will be a lasting effect of the pandemic (Gesi et al., 2020). To highlight one such complication, countless individuals had to say goodbye to dying loved ones over technologies like FaceTime or, similarly, attend funerals (if they could be held at all) via Zoom without the ability to have tangible physical support; it will likely take much time—perhaps decades—before the full effects that the pandemic has had on our personal sense of grief are fully understood (Purdum, 2020).

Over the past several decades—at least since the pioneering work of Kübler-Ross' (1969) classic five stages of grief model—many clinicians and scholars from psychology and related fields have tried to classify or categorize grief. Without getting much mired into that history, one such way to look at loss was suggested by psychologist Therese Rando (1993) who suggested (in a broad sense) that grief could either be physical or symbolic in nature. Physical loss, like the death of a loved one, is almost more plainly tangible to realize that someone or something that was once there is no more, whereas symbolic loss can be a more subtle (but still just as potentially painful) form of loss that may not be as tangibly realized by others or oneself (such as a loss of status in one's job). Early in the pandemic, in April 2020, Weir (2020) provided some guidance from some noted psychologists who specialize in grief about what that moment may mean and how to move forward—with a particular focus on some of the more subtle symbolic (or ambiguous) losses that virtually all of us have experienced in the pandemic—and an understanding that we are all sharing a "collective" sense of grief and that it is important to simply first acknowledge that point. As a noted grief scholar, Dr. George Bonanno, put it:

> Grief is really about turning inward and recalibrating, and thinking: 'This is not the way the world is anymore, and I need to adapt…It's okay to feel grief over what we're losing. When we do that, it allows us to let grief do its job, so that we can move on (Weir, 2020, p. 2).

Another important scholar to the field, Dr. Robert Neimeyer added:

> The losses [from the pandemic] include our sense of predictability, control, justice, and the belief that we can protect our children or elderly loved ones…We're capable of losing places, projects, possessions, and protections, all of which we may be powerfully attached to…This pandemic forces us to confront the frailty of such attachment, whether it's to our local bookstore or the routines that sustain us through our days…We're [also] talking about grieving a living loss—one that keeps going and going…[But o]ne thing about crisis is that it can galvanize creativity and commitment…Psychology has a purpose and direction in this crisis that is quite clear. We can retreat from it, or we can embrace that moment (Weir, 2020, pp. 2, 4).

A review of nearly three dozen articles by Kumar (2021) suggests that it is important to consider both the differing developmental issues and complicating factors of grief (e.g., primary and secondary stressors) related to the pandemic. This analysis further noted that Covid has largely fomented four broad categories of grief which have been explored in this book. Some of the more personal components of Covid-related grief involved either grief for oneself (e.g., loss of life events or milestones or employment) or relational grief (often, though not exclusively, involving death). Two broader categories of grief involved a more communal grief for what society has lost as well as an ecological grief related to concerns over the environment. Indeed, at the two-year-end mark of the pandemic, the amount and level of sustained potential trauma that Americans have been subjected to has truly tested our general coping skills (Iati, 2021).

To sum up, as might be expected, psychological resilience and coping with the perceived stress of Covid appears to be important for maintaining well-being (e.g., Peker & Cengiz, 2022). But, to return to the TED talk from Dr. Wernicke, she ends it by saying: "…if we can invest in more solutions to loneliness to create a culture of mental health and if as individuals we can commit to creating a culture of inclusion by sharing and embracing all of our stories especially if they're about mental illness then we can save even more lives" (Wernicke, 2021, 12:05). Even if our general state of well-being and adjustment largely returns to pre-pandemic functioning as might be predicted from earlier psychological literature (e.g., Brickman et al., 1978), the Covid pandemic will be replete with stories where many of them are laced with loss, grief, or mental health challenges; many of the tellers of these stories may find some solace and strength in not just sharing them but having sympathetic listeners as well.

References

Barth, F. D. (2021, January 1). It's hard to be optimistic after surviving trauma, but it's not impossible. Here's how to start. *NBC News*. https://www.nbcnews.com/think/opinion/it-s-hard-be-optimistic-after-surviving-trauma-it-s-ncna1252611

Bignardi, G., Dalmaijer, E. S., Anwyl-Irvine, A. L., Smith, T. A., Siugzdaite, R., Uh, S., & Astle, D. E. (2021). Longitudinal increases in childhood depression symptoms during the COVID-19 lockdown. *Archives of Disease in Childhood, 106*(8), 791-797. http://dx.doi.org/10.1136/archdischild-2020-320372

Brickman, P., Coates, D., & Janoff-Bulman, R. (1978). Lottery winners and accident victims: Is happiness relative? *Journal of Personality and Social Psychology, 36*(8), 917–927. https://doi.org/10.1037/0022-3514.36.8.917

Brooks, A. C. (2020, September 24). What to do when the future feels hopeless. *The Atlantic*. https://www.theatlantic.com/family/archive/2020/09/what-do-when-future-feels-hopeless/616448/

Carloss, T. (2020, October 27/28). 2020 taking toll on American's mental health. *ABC News 5 Cleveland*. https://www.news5cleveland.com/news/local-news/2020-taking-toll-on-americans-mental-health

Demopoulos, A. (2020, September 26). Mental health chief: There is 'no doubt' people will suffer coronavirus 'PTSD'. *The Daily Beast*. https://www.thedailybeast.com/mental-health-chief-says-there-is-no-doubt-people-will-suffer-coronavirus-ptsd

Edelman, H. [@hope_edelman] (2021, December 30). *2020 gave me a #divorce, a pandemic, the near collapse of my company, an empty nest, and having to sell* [Tweet]. Twitter. https://twitter.com/hope_edelman/status/1344478655997624320?s=20

Eisenstein, P. A. (2021, April 7). 'Zoom zombies' are zoning out behind the wheel after video calls, auto safety experts warn. *NBC News*. https://www.nbcnews.com/business/autos/zoom-zombies-are-zoning-out-behind-wheel-after-video-calls-n1263367

Fowers, A., & Wan, W. (2020, May 26). A third of Americans now show signs of clinical anxiety or depression, Census Bureau finds amid coronavirus pandemic. *The Washington Post*. https://www.washingtonpost.com/health/2020/05/26/americans-with-depression-anxiety-pandemic/

Gesi, C., Carmassi, C., Cerveri, G., Carpita, B., Cremone, I. M., & Dell'Osso, L. (2020). Complicated grief: What to expect after the coronavirus pandemic. *Frontiers in Psychiatry, 11,* 489. https://doi.org/10.3389/fpsyt.2020.00489

Graff, G. M. (2020, September 10). The grief Americans no longer share. *The Atlantic.* https://www.theatlantic.com/ideas/archive/2020/09/america-loses-its-capacity-common-grief/616234/

Grant, A. (2021, April 19/December 3). There's a name for the blah you're feeling: It's called languishing. *The New York Times.* https://www.nytimes.com/2021/04/19/well/mind/covid-mental-health-languishing.html

Harvey, J. H. (2000). *Give sorrow words: Perspectives on loss and trauma.* Taylor & Francis.

Iati, M. (2021, December 24). Bracing for the next phase of the coronavirus recession: Bankruptcies. *The Washington Post.* https://www.washingtonpost.com/health/2021/12/24/collective-trauma-public-outbursts/

Kübler-Ross. (1969). *On death and dying.* Collier.

Kumar, R. M. (2021). The many faces of grief: A systematic literature review of grief during the COVID-19 Pandemic. *Illness, Crisis & Loss.* 105413732110380 84. https://doi.org/10.1177/10541373211038084

Melore, C. (2021, January 8). 2020 was so bad, 1 in 6 Americans entered therapy for the first time! *Study Finds.* https://www.studyfinds.org/2020-so-bad-americans-entered-therapy-first-time/

Nemo, L. (2020, May 1). How the coronavirus pandemic is warping our sense of time. *Discover.* https://www.discovermagazine.com/mind/how-the-coronavirus-pandemic-is-warping-our-sense-of-time

Norcross, J. C., & Phillips, C. M. (2020). Psychologist self-care during the pandemic: Now more than ever. *Journal of Health Service Psychology, 46,* 59-63. https://doi.org/10.1007/s42843-020-00010-5

Park, C. L., Russell, B. S., Fendrich, M., Finkelstein-Fox, L., Hutchison, M., & Becker, J. (2020). Americans' COVID-19 stress, coping, and adherence to CDC guidelines. *Journal of General Internal Medicine, 35*(8), 2296-2303. https://doi.org/ 10.1007/s11606-020-05898-9

Peker, A., & Cengiz, S. (2022). Covid-19 fear, happiness and stress in adults: The mediating role of psychological resilience and coping with stress. *International Journal of Psychiatry in Clinical Practice, 26*(2), 123-131. https://doi.org/10.10 80/13651501.2021.1937656

Purdum, T. S. (2020, December 9). Drive-by burials and FaceTime farewells: Grief in the Covid era will weigh on the American psyche for years to come. *STAT.* https://www.statnews.com/2020/12/09/drive-by-burials-and-facetime-farewells-grief-in-the-covid-era-will-weigh-on-the-american-psyche-for-years-to-come/

Rando, T. A. (1993). *Treatment of complicated mourning.* Research Press.

Ray, J. (2021, July 20). 2020 sets records for negative emotions. *Gallup News.* https://news.gallup.com/poll/352205/2020-sets-records-negative-emotions.aspx

Sapolsky, R. M. (2020, August 22). Why our brains are having so much trouble with Covid-19. *CNN.* https://www.cnn.com/2020/08/22/opinions/covid-19-mental-health-sapolsky/index.html

Sarner, M. (2021, April 14). Brain fog: How trauma, uncertainty and isolation have affected our minds and memory. *The Guardian.* https://www.theguardian.com/lifeandstyle/2021/apr/14/brain-fog-how-trauma-uncertainty-and-isolation-have-affected-our-minds-and-memory

Seow, S. (2020, October 10/27). Therapists predict how this year will shape our mental health. *HuffPost.* https://www.huffpost.com/entry/therapists-2020-mental-health_l_5f7dda48c5b6fc1dec78790a

Shklarski, L., Abrams, A., & Bakst, E. (2021). Navigating changes in the physical and psychological spaces of psychotherapists during Covid-19: When home becomes the office. *Practice Innovations, 6*(1), 55–66. https://doi.org/10.1037/pri0000138.

Siemaszko, C. (2020, December 21). Many will be missing from holiday tables this year. Traditions help with coping. *NBC News.* https://www.nbcnews.com/news/us-news/many-will-be-missing-holiday-tables-year-traditions-help-coping-n1250262?icid=related

Stroebe, M., & Schut, H. (2021). Bereavement in times of COVID-19: A review and theoretical framework. *OMEGA-Journal of Death and Dying, 82(3),* 500–522. https://doi.org/10.1177/0030222820966928

Thomas, N., & Romano, S. (2020, October 12). A 'second wave' of mental health devastation due to Covid-19 is imminent, experts say. *CNN.* https://www.cnn.com/2020/10/12/health/mental-health-second-wave-coronavirus-wellness/index.html

Weir, K. (2020, April 1). Grief and COVID-19: Mourning our bygone lives. *American Psychological Association.* https://www.apa.org/news/apa/2020/grief-covid-19

Wernicke, R. (2021, April). *Mental health in the new normal: Shaping our COVID stories* [Video]. TED Conferences. https://www.ted.com/talks/dr_rachel_wernicke_mental_health_in_the_new_normal_shaping_our_covid_stories

CHAPTER SIX

Challenges to Select Populations

While the Covid pandemic impacted the lives of individuals across the world, in America, certain populations had to contend with select and unique additional challenges. As such, this chapter highlights some of the issues that may have been caused or exacerbated by the pandemic with respect to considerations of the elderly and those with compromised health conditions, race, caregiving burdens, and the homeless.

The Elderly and Those with Compromised Health Conditions

This chapter explores some select populations who may have faced unique challenges in the pandemic even though there was a general sense (well before Covid) that a pandemic had the potential to impact large segments of a population globally (even if there have been varying scientific definitions of what exactly constitutes a pandemic; Morens et al., 2009). While Covid was largely thought to not impact the young, as of mid-December 2021, it was estimated that over 1,000 children in the United States had been killed by Covid (Dutton, 2021). Moreover, the question of why sometimes even young and seemingly healthy adults had fallen very ill—or even died—has been a lingering mystery from the earliest days of the pandemic; though, it does appear that the presence of either certain autoantibodies, a pro-inflammatory protein, or genes may help to answer this question (Chalmers & Blanchard, 2021; Gower, 2021). And, the reasons why some individuals experience so-called "long Covid" remains not entirely clear at the time of this writing; in such instances, physical, mental, and social symptoms (such as cough, headache, and cognitive decline) can persist in patients for weeks (or months) following even a relatively mild Covid infection (e.g., van Kessel et al., 2022).

However, as suggested initially in the pandemic—and further documented later (e.g., Bhaskaran et al., 2021)—older age was a significant risk factor for heightened mortality (along with other health comorbidities and being of male sex or a member of a non-white racial or ethnic group). The CDC (2022) further corroborated and summarized much of this evidence that being elderly or having certain comorbidities (including, but not limited to, obesity, cancer, heart disease, and chronic lung diseases) put individuals at much greater risk of becoming very ill or dying from the virus. While advanced age and health comorbidities should not necessarily be viewed as interchangeable or inherent realities, there is much evidence to support the importance of considering the role of age-related comorbidities when determining one's potential Covid risk (Antos et al., 2021).

To expand on the previous point in a slightly different way, even though Covid represented a theoretical threat to everyone from the beginning of the pandemic, it was increasingly clear that the elderly and those with select health conditions (regardless of age) were likely facing the greatest health risks from the virus. And yet, there has been some conflicting evidence as to whether either advanced age or the presence of higher-risk health conditions, in and of themselves, were direct predictors of fear of Covid infection (e.g., Yadav et al., 2021; Quadros et al., 2021). In fact, Patra (2021) suggests that elderly individuals who were medically and psychiatrically fit not only coped well during the pandemic but also showed much resilience (e.g., by regulating emotions, showing cognitive flexibility, and engaging in a healthy lifestyle).

But still, in addition to the physical concerns associated with the virus, many seniors have felt that the pandemic upended and disrupted how they planned to spend the latter part of their lives and that this lost time represents time that cannot be reclaimed or recovered (Kuriloff, 2021). And yet, though the pandemic may have exacerbated feelings of loss and loneliness amongst the elderly (e.g., Bhutani & Greenwald, 2021), younger adults may also have experienced such feelings, particularly given the profound disruptions that the pandemic has created for their lives (which is often built around forging social connections; Beam & Kim, 2020).

Though more research is needed to further flesh out these points, it may well be that one's pre-existing health and medical conditions (perhaps coupled with advanced age) may have been an even greater predictor of psychological distress and challenges in regard to coping with the pandemic. For instance, older adults with cancer were particularly concerned with contracting Covid and dealing with feelings of isolation (Verma et al., 2022). In a different study, Smith and colleagues (2021) found that while over half of a large sample of healthcare workers screened positive for the presence of traumatic stress, depression, or anxiety, mental health risks were particularly enhanced for those workers who were immunocompromised or had an immunocompromised household member. To offer some additional context, it is important to be mindful of the fact that about 60% of Americans were believed to have some underlying health condition that could increase their Covid risk—including the more than 40% of Americans who are classified as being obese (Radcliffe, 2020). And, indeed, there was evidence that the pandemic was associated with an increase in reported stress and loneliness among the obese (Borgatti et al., 2022).

Race and Health Disparities

Social scientists and others have long documented many significant health disparities that have existed throughout much of U.S. history, including (but not limited to) lower life expectancy at birth and greater prevalence of chronic health conditions like hypertension and diabetes faced by racial minorities in comparison to whites (Williams & Sternthal, 2010). While many factors may explain these disparities, stereotype threat—where minorities have to contend with the negative stereotypes about their group—may further foment these disparities (Aronson et al., 2013).

Consistent with these points, one of the more disturbing realities of the pandemic has been the disproportionate number of African-Americans, Hispanic Americans, Native Americans, and Asian Americans who have died which highlights both economic and health care disparities in the United States (Flagg et al., 2020). Asian-Americans, in particular, were at particular risk of increased posttraumatic stress disorder (PTSD) symptomology when controlling for pre-existing physical and mental health factors as a function of the pervasive Covid-related discrimination experienced by this racial group during the pandemic (Hahm et al., 2021). Hahm and colleagues (2022) found evidence of three broad types of anti-Asian discrimination: societal (linked with political discrimination), interpersonal (in the form of both overt and covert direct discrimination and vicarious discrimination, both in person and online), and intrapersonal (or internalized) discrimination. Unfortunately, racial and ethnic disparities in health and health care have been well-documented as being quite pervasive long before the pandemic (e.g., Sue & Dhindsa, 2006). The question of what exactly constitutes such disparities is often fraught with controversy, in part, given the potential to inaccurately portray such differences as well as the influence of how social class and socioeconomic factors are pertinent (Adler & Rehkopf, 2008). Regarding the latter point, for all of the importance placed on trying to minimize the spread and risk of infection of the virus by perhaps telecommuting, only about a quarter of employed Americans were able to do so every day in August 2020—but significantly fewer African-American (9.4%) and Hispanic (19.2%) workers were able to do so during this same time period (Schmidt, 2020). It is also important to emphasize that those who lived in urban areas and, particularly, those with higher educational attainment were more likely to be able to work from home (which also represents another form of societal divide; Fox, 2020). And, perhaps not unsurprisingly, those with greater wealth were generally more apt and able to socially distance, particularly at the height of the initial lockdowns; by contrast, poorer individuals and essential workers often were not able to do so (Simon, 2020).

Many scholars, such as Yearby (2020), have argued that social factors and inadequate access to health-related resources are often rooted in structural racism. Bajaj and Stanford (2021) noted that a survey from the National Association for the Advancement of Colored People (NAACP) in late November 2020 found that (at that time) only 14% of the African-American respondents trusted the safety of the Covid vaccine and only 18% were planning to definitely get vaccinated. In their analysis, these authors discuss the infamous Tuskegee Syphilis Study where hundreds of African-American men were followed in a study—without giving their informed consent—for about 40 years and not offering treatment for their syphilis even though it was available. However, Bajaj and Stanford (2021) contend that it is likely not the recollection of this (and related) deeply unethical study per se (and the institutional racism from medical history) that produced such initial wariness about Covid treatments but rather the personal challenges faced by African-Americans in navigating health care institutions. Lin et al. (2022) largely echo these points by noting not just the historical and perceived realities of these racial inequalities, but also how vaccine hesitancy can be due to a number of logistical and information barriers, including transportation, inability to take time off from work or find convenient sites, and misinformation.

On May 25, 2020—little more than two months following the initial surge of the pandemic—an event occurred that was widely viewed as a "racial reckoning." African-American George Floyd was murdered by a police officer—with three other officers looking on and involved in the infraction—kneeling on his neck for over 8 minutes while screaming "I can't breathe" with the incident being videotaped on a cell phone. This event would trigger worldwide protests described as the largest since the Civil Rights Movement and gave greater prominence and support to the Black Lives Matter movement—even if it was sometimes perceived differently as a function of race (Sinclair & Starck, 2021). But, it is arguable—and perhaps even questionable (e.g., Onwuachi-Willig, 2021)—as to whether the George Floyd killing has resulted in longer-term cultural trauma, particularly for whites.

Though the murder of George Floyd and the ensuing protests raises a bevy of critical issues, in regard to its role in the pandemic, there may be at least two issues particularly worth highlighting. Given that the U.S. was in the earliest stages of the pandemic where social gatherings were discouraged, some concern was noted as to whether these mass protests contributed to viral spread—though initial reports suggested that they largely did not (Lopez, 2020). Subsequent research did find a statistically significant but very small increase in Covid cases following the protests (Neyman & Dalsey, 2021). However, at the time of these protests, many physicians particularly argued that the health risks and harms associated with the pernicious effects of systemic racism far outweighed any Covid-related considerations (Ducharme, 2020). Frankly, the murder of George Floyd, along with Covid's disproportionate toll on U.S. populations of color, was often viewed as a breaking point symptom of historical underlying structural racism in America (Krieger, 2020).

Perhaps an even more provocative question to consider is whether the dynamics of the pandemic itself, in some way, contributed to the mass protests that erupted following George Floyd's death. Several analyses at the time of these protests did indeed suggest that the pandemic was at least a contributing factor. Cheung (2020) noted that there had been several other high profile cases involving the deaths of African Americans at the hands of the police (such as Eric Garner, Michael Brown, and Tamir Rice), but none of these triggered the more sustained, widespread, and diverse protests as did Floyd's murder. As Cheung (2020) suggests, the pandemic could have somehow been implicated whether it be due to (direct or indirect) stress related to it (including financial) or the particularly egregious means by which Floyd died—which was widely viewed (particularly at the time when stay at home orders were still widespread). Arguably, there were many factors—some of which may not have necessarily been linked to the pandemic per se—such as the vast amount of footage of the murder (which was also widely circulated via social media)—that may have contributed to why Floyd's murder produced such mass protests in contrast to some of the other aforementioned high profile killings of African-Americans; even so, both direct and indirect consequences of the pandemic likely helped to fuel much of these reactions (Christián et al., 2022). Political scientist Maneesh Arora (2020) argues that Floyd's killing may have been akin to a final straw for those experiencing financial distress and after many African-Americans had already been experiencing disproportionately adverse effects related to the pandemic. Altman (2020) furthers many of these aforesaid themes while adding that the protests also were a means to showcase outrage against many of then-President Trump's racial and ethnic divisions.

While the George Floyd protests were almost universally supported by most public health officials as a means of expressing the rage of systemic racism, there were some (particularly conservatives and others who raised objections over lockdown orders) who seriously questioned the perceived fairness and inconsistency of supporting the Floyd protests if the overarching goal (at the time) was to prevent viral spread (Weiner, 2020). As an example, during the protests, a Republican State representative, tweeted: "social distancing is critical to stop the spread of COVID-19 — unless you have a great photo op ... I'll take hypocrisy for $1000." (Weiner, 2020, p. 2). Tom Frieden, the CDC director during the Obama administration, noted that many viewed him as hypocritical for supporting the protests during a pandemic, but he added that since most protests were outdoors, they were safer. He further cautioned: "The broader issue is really an issue of trust in government. If that trust is undermined by violent policing, or it's undermined by ham-handed public health actions that don't respect communities, that's going to have a negative impact on our ability to fight disease" (Weiner, 2020, p. 3). Of course, it is very difficult to distinguish those who may have voiced concerns over hypocrisy regarding the protests from those who may have stated such complaints to couch their opposition to the protesters as well.

Nonetheless, like many of the consequences and effects of the pandemic, it is impossible to state with certainty the precise causal factors behind the mass protests. Sometimes extreme events can allow people en masse to rise up against evil or injustice, such as in fighting against war or genocide (e.g., Staub, 2003). Another profound contemporary example can be shown by the Ukrainian resistance against the 2022 Russian invasion (e.g., Graham-Harrison, 2022). Perhaps the George Floyd protests also represented such an event (even if we may never know its precise causal origins). It may be more important to consider its longer-term effects on highlighting, addressing, and correcting racial disparities. A study of select race-related Tweets from November 2019 through September 2020 suggested that negatively-themed messages referencing Black people decreased for a few weeks following Floyd's murder—but this was short-lived; these researchers further concluded that negative attitudes towards Black people remained deeply entrenched in society (Nguyen et al., 2021). Even so, there remains hope that the current and future generations of children will continue to find the value of fighting for justice in the spirit of the George Floyd protests (Dreyer et al., 2020).

Caregiving Burdens

As considered in Chapter 4, most couples and families faced many great challenges during the pandemic. Well before the pandemic, caregiving could take many forms—from the care of children to the care of elderly or sick family members—and it has been shown to be a predictor for the potential of strain and burnout, including various psychiatric and physical morbidity effects (e.g., Schulz et al., 1990). Though women have often traditionally been associated with expectations of caregiving responsibilities, men and women often experience different sources of stress when carrying out such actions (Swinkels et al., 2019); these researchers add that women's overall greater partner caregiving burden may be more related to secondary issues (such as relational or financial problems) whereas caregiving intensity poses a greater burden for men. However, other reviews and related analyses have found many gender-related caregiving burdens to be relatively small in magnitude (e.g., Pinquart & Sörensen, 2006; Sharma et al., 2016).

The pandemic may have exacerbated some of these caregiving trends (Beach et al., 2021). Stefanova et al. (2021) offer evidence that there was a significant gender imbalance in households (from a worldwide sample conducted in mid-May through early July 2020) such that women were more likely to tend to caregiving tasks and significantly less time on work—typically to the detriment of their work—in contrast to their male partners (who did not show like behaviors). However, another investigation with an entirely American sample conducted in early June 2020 was largely consistent with many of the earlier studies, which found that women had higher levels of caregiving burden, but men with a higher level of caregiving intensity reported increased caregiving burdens (Cohen et al., 2021).

As further considered in Chapter 9, Internet use during the pandemic offered a mix of benefits and challenges to caregivers as well. In many respects, the pandemic presented the ultimate culmination of the blur between work-life balance. While many parents and caregivers were able to work from home—which could be a potential benefit—we also know that trying to juggle the demands of work and caregiving simultaneously is often a great burden in and of itself (e.g., Wang et al., 2022). In many cases, the Internet may have been a critical lifeline allowing caregivers to help their older or medically fragile parents or family members to still receive care or assistance in various forms; however, cyber-based caregiving (e.g., providing care via digital technologies) also posed its own challenges as well such as not having the necessary digital skills to successfully navigate such technologies (e.g., Gallistl et al., 2021).

Despite some of these broader caregiving concerns emanating from—or exacerbated by—the pandemic, it does appear that the pandemic has likely widened some gender disparities in the American workforce. According to data from the Pew Research Center, women with a high school education or less were significantly less represented in the workforce in 2021 than two years prior, whereas women with at least a bachelor's degree actually showed a modest increase during this same time period; while it is difficult to absolutely account for this disparity, it is often presumed that such women were overrepresented in certain health care and service occupations that were initially curtailed during the start of the pandemic and were more likely to require on-site work (which may have been further complicated by limited child care and schooling options; Fry, 2022). Stevenson (2021) adds that women who felt pressure to work in potentially dangerous conditions may have also left jobs particularly given not just increased parenting demands but also increased eldercare responsibilities (and related threats of potential viral transmission).

The Homeless

It is also well-known that homelessness is associated with a host of increased risk for both physical and mental illness (Martens, 2001). Poor hygienic conditions may have also posed a greater challenge for this population and, consistent with the previous point about increased morbidity risk, it should not be surprising that in one small study conducted between March and May 2020 of homeless individuals in Germany, nearly two-thirds of that sample met the criteria for a DSM-5 psychiatric disorder (Hajek, 2022). And yet, Marcus et al. (2021) correctly point out that not only is there no clear causal relationship between mental illness and homelessness, there are a variety of complex social, financial, and psychological factors that can contribute to its occurrence—many of which may have particularly taxed some individuals (including some facing homelessness for the first time in their life) during the pandemic.

The homeless represented yet another group uniquely impacted by the pandemic. Naturally, particularly during the initial (and subsequent) surges, homeless individuals lacked an obvious place to shelter in place during this threat. For both their own protection as well as the interest of larger public health concerns, this was another concern that highlighted the necessity of appropriate local and federal responses (Benavides & Nukpezah, 2020). However, even assurances of such shelter could not necessarily protect against viral outbreaks within such sites, which highlighted the importance of both mass testing and isolation (Chang et al., 2022).

Attempting to ascertain how the pandemic has impacted the state of homelessness in America is a challenging question that will require continued attention. While homelessness did increase in 2020 over the previous year—it had been increasing for the previous three years as well and about a quarter of all homeless individuals were located in either New York City or Los Angeles (Fessler, 2021). Indeed, homelessness in New York City increased by at least 3% from March to September 2020, with a corresponding 72% increase in complaint phone calls to its "311" non-emergency number where both the city and its citizens grew increasingly wary of increased homeless encampments that popped up since the pandemic (ABC News 7, 2020). But, some further caution is also needed when interpreting such trends as homelessness did not universally increase in all major U.S. cities and homelessness is also considered to be a lagging indicator of housing distress (Ring & Schuetz, 2021). More broadly though, as is the case with most sectors in society, the pandemic has likely altered the dimensions of homelessness that has highlighted (among other issues) the growing need for more affordable and diverse housing (O'Flaherty, 2022).

In many respects, the pandemic exacerbated many of the well-documented burdens and challenges that are often encountered by members of the populations discussed in this chapter. This chapter is also an important reminder that many other extremely significant events took place during the earliest phases of the pandemic, such as the tragic murder of George Floyd. As was previously discussed, while it would be erroneous to suggest that such significant events— like Floyd's death and the ensuing mass protests against it—were necessarily directly caused by the pandemic, it would seem fairly accurate to suggest that it was at least a factor that fueled the protests. This chapter also serves as a reminder of the importance of appreciating and working to ameliorate the challenges faced by many in these populations.

References

ABC News 7. (2020, September 22). 7 On Your Side: Coronavirus pandemic puts spotlight on NYC homelessness crisis. *ABC News 7.* https://abc7ny.com/new-york-city-homeless-7-on-your-side-investigates-nyc-311-calls/6431714/

Adler, N. E., & Rehkopf, D. H. (2008). US disparities in health: Descriptions, causes, and mechanisms. *Annual Review of Public Health, 29,* 235-252. https://doi.org/10.1146/annurev.publhealth.29.020907.090852

Altman, A. (2020, June 4). Why the killing of George Floyd sparked an American uprising. *Time.* https://time.com/5847967/george-floyd-protests-trump/

Antos, A., Kwong, M. L., Balmorez, T., Villanueva, A., & Murakami, S. (2021). Unusually high risks of COVID-19 mortality with age-related comorbidities: An adjusted meta-analysis method to improve the risk assessment of mortality using the comorbid mortality data. *Infectious Disease Reports, 13*(3), 700-711. https://doi.org/10.3390/idr13030065

Aronson, J., Burgess, D., Phelan, S. M., & Juarez, L. (2013). Unhealthy interactions: The role of stereotype threat in health disparities. *American Journal of Public Health, 103*(1), 50-56. https://doi.org/10.2105/AJPH.2012.300828

Arora, M. (2020, August 5). How the coronavirus pandemic helped the Floyd protests become the biggest in U.S. history. *The Washington Post.* https://www.washingtonpost.com/politics/2020/08/05/how-coronavirus-pandemic-helped-floyd-protests-become-biggest-us-history/

Bajaj, S. S., & Stanford, F. C. (2021). Beyond Tuskegee—vaccine distrust and everyday racism. *New England Journal of Medicine, 384*(5), e12. https://doi.org/10.1056/NEJMpv2035827

Beach, S. R., Schulz, R., Donovan, H., & Rosland, A. M. (2021). Family caregiving during the COVID-19 pandemic. *The Gerontologist, 61*(5), 650-660. https://doi.org/10.1093/geront/gnab049

Beam, C. R., & Kim, A. J. (2020). Psychological sequelae of social isolation and loneliness might be a larger problem in young adults than older adults. *Psychological Trauma: Theory, Research, Practice, and Policy, 12*(S1), S58-S60. http://dx.doi.org/10.1037/tra0000774

Benavides, A. D., & Nukpezah, J. A. (2020). How local governments are caring for the homeless during the COVID-19 pandemic. *The American Review of*

Public Administration, 50(6-7), 650-657. https://doi.org/10.1177/0275074020 942062

Bhaskaran, K., Bacon, S., Evans, S. J., Bates, C. J., Rentsch, C. T., MacKenna, B., Tomlinson, L., Walker, A. J., Schultze, A., Morton, C. E., Grint, D., Mehrkar, A., Eggo, R. M., Inglesby, P., Douglas, I. J., McDonald, H. I., Cockburn, J., Williamson, E. J., Evans, D., ... Goldacre, B. (2021). Factors associated with deaths due to COVID-19 versus other causes: Population-based cohort analysis of UK primary care data and linked national death registrations within the OpenSAFELY platform. *The Lancet Regional Health-Europe, 6*, 100109. https://doi.org/10.1016/j. lanepe.2021.100109

Bhutani, S., & Greenwald, B. (2021). Loneliness in the elderly during the COVID-19 pandemic: A literature review in preparation for a future study. *The American Journal of Geriatric Psychiatry, 29*(4), S87-S88. https://doi.org/10. 1016/j.jagp.2021.01.081

Borgatti, A. C., Crockett, K. B., Jacob, A. E., Davis, A. L., & Dutton, G. R. (2022). Correlates of psychological distress among adults with obesity during the COVID-19 pandemic. *Psychology & Health*, 1-18. https://doi.org/10.1080/088 70446.2022.2038790

CDC. (2022, February 15). Underlying medical conditions associated with higher risk for severe COVID-19: Information for healthcare professionals. *The Centers for Disease Control and Prevention.* https://www.cdc.gov/coronavirus/ 2019-ncov/hcp/clinical-care/underlyingconditions.html

Chalmers, V., & Blanchard, S. (2021, November 4/5). Scientists solve the mystery of why Covid kills some people and not others. *The U. S. Sun.* https://www. the-sun.com/health/4000041/why-covid-kills-some-people-not-others/

Chang, Y. S., Mayer, S., Davis, E. S., Figueroa, E., Leo, P., Finn, P. W., & Perkins, D. L. (2022). Transmission dynamics of large coronavirus disease outbreak in homeless shelter, Chicago, Illinois, USA, 2020. *Emerging Infectious Diseases, 28*(1), 76-84. https://doi.org/10.3201/eid2801.210780

Cheung, H. (2020, June 8). George Floyd death: Why US protests are so powerful this time. *BBC News.* https://www.bbc.com/news/world-us-canada-52969905

Christián, L., Erdős, Á., & Háló, G. (2022). The background and repercussions of the George Floyd case. *Cogent Social Sciences, 8*(1), 1-17. https://doi.org/10. 1080/23311886.2022.2082094

Cohen, S. A., Kunicki, Z. J., Drohan, M. M., & Greaney, M. L. (2021). Exploring changes in caregiver burden and caregiving intensity due to COVID-19. *Gerontology and Geriatric Medicine, 7.* https://doi.org/10.1177/2333721421999279

Dreyer, B. P., Trent, M., Anderson, A. T., Askew, G. L., Boyd, R., Coker, T. R., Coyne-Beasley, T., Fuentes-Afflick, E., Johnson, T., Mendoza, F., Montoya Williams, D., Oyeka, S. O., Poitevien, P., Spinks-Franklin, A. A. I., Thomas, O. W., Walker-Harding, L., Willis, E., Wright, J. L., Berman, S., ... Stein, F. (2020). The death of George Floyd: Bending the arc of history toward justice for generations of children. *Pediatrics, 146*(3), e2020009639. https:// doi.org/10.15 42/peds.2020-009639

Ducharme, J. (2020, June 10). 'Protest is a profound public health intervention.' Why so many doctors are supporting protests in the middle of the COVID-19 pandemic. *Time.* https://time.com/5848212/doctors-supporting-protests/

Dutton, J. (2021, December 16). Over 1,000 children in U.S. have been killed by COVID. *Newsweek*. https://www.newsweek.com/over-1000-children-u-s-killed-covid-1660124

Fessler, P. (2021, March 18). HUD: Growth of homelessness during 2020 was 'devastating,' even before the pandemic. *NPR*. https://www.npr.org/2021/03/18/978244891/hud-growth-of-homelessness-during-2020-was-devastating-even-before-the-pandemic

Flagg, A., Sharma, D., Fenn, L., & Stobbe, M. (2020, August 21). COVID-19's toll on people of color is worse than we know. *The Marshall Project*. https://www.themarshallproject.org/2020/08/21/covid-19-s-toll-on-people-of-color-is-worse-than-we-knew

Fox, J. (2020, October 5/6). Who's still working at home? You, probably. *Bloomberg*. https://www.bloombergquint.com/opinion/working-from-home-adds-pain-to-pandemic-economy

Fry, R. (2022, January 14). Some gender disparities widened in the U.S. workforce during the pandemic. *Pew Research Center*. https://www.pewresearch.org/fact-tank/2022/01/14/some-gender-disparities-widened-in-the-u-s-workforce-during-the-pandemic/

Gallistl, V., Seifert, A., & Kolland, F. (2021). COVID-19 as a "digital push?" Research experiences from long-term care and recommendations for the post-pandemic era. *Frontiers in Public Health*, 9, 660064. https://doi.org/10.3389/fpubh.2021.660064

Gower, T. (2021, May 4). Why some die, some survive when equally ill from COVID-19. *The Harvard Gazette*. https://news.harvard.edu/gazette/story/2021/05/researchers-identify-protein-signature-in-severe-covid-19-cases/

Graham-Harrison, E. (2022, February 23). Ukrainians ready for resistance: 'The whole country will be fighting back'. *The Guardian*. https://www.theguardian.com/world/2022/feb/23/ukrainians-ready-for-resistance-the-whole-country-will-be-fighting-back

Hahm, H. C., Ha, Y., Scott, J. C., Wongchai, V., Chen, J. A., & Liu, C. H. (2021). Perceived COVID-19-related anti-Asian discrimination predicts post traumatic stress disorder symptoms among Asian and Asian American young adults. *Psychiatry Research*, 303, 114084. https://doi.org/10.1016/j.psychres.2021.114084

Hahm, H. C., Xavier Hall, C. D., Garcia, K. T., Cavallino, A., Ha, Y., Cozier, Y. C., & Liu, C. (2021). Experiences of COVID-19-related anti-Asian discrimination and affective reactions in a multiple race sample of US young adults. *BMC Public Health*, 21(1), 1-11. https://doi.org/10.1186/s12889-021-11559-1

Hajek, A., Heinrich, F., van Rüth, V., Kretzler, B., Langenwalder, F., Püschel, K., Bertram, F., & König, H. H. (2022) Prevalence and determinants of depression and anxiety measured by the PHQ-4 among homeless individuals during the COVID-19 pandemic. Evidence from the Hamburg survey of homeless individuals. *Psychiatry Research*, 308, 114350. https://doi.org/10.1016/j.psychres.2021.114350

Krieger, N. (2020). ENOUGH: COVID-19, structural racism, police brutality, plutocracy, climate change—and time for health justice, democratic governance, and an equitable, sustainable future. *American Journal of Public Health*, 110(11), 1620-1623. https://doi.org/10.2105/AJPH.2020.305886

Kuriloff, P. (2021, February 7). Covid gives seniors another reason to mourn: The shadow it's cast on our golden years. *NBC News*. https://www.nbcnews.com/

think/opinion/covid-gives-seniors-another-reason-mourn-shadow-it-s-cast-ncna1256917

Lin, C., Tu, P., & Terry, T. C. (2022). Moving the needle on racial disparity: COVID-19 vaccine trust and hesitancy. *Vaccine, 40*(1), 5-8. https://doi.org/10.1016/j.vaccine.2021.11.010

Lopez, G. (2020, June 26). The effect of Black Lives Matter protests on coronavirus cases, explained. *Vox.* https://www.vox.com/2020/6/26/21300636/coronavirus-pandemic-black-lives-matter-protests

Marcus, L., Johnson, C., & Ramirez, D. (2021, May 21). The complex link between homelessness and mental health. *Psychology Today.* https://www.psychology today.com/us/blog/mind-matters-menninger/202105/the-complex-link-between-homelessness-and-mental-health

Martens, W. H. (2001). A review of physical and mental health in homeless persons. *Public Health Reviews, 29*(1), 13-33.

Morens, D. M., Folkers, G. K., & Fauci, A. S. (2009). What is a pandemic? *The Journal of Infectious Diseases, 200*(7), 1018-1021.

Neyman, G., & Dalsey, W. (2021). Black Lives Matter protests and COVID-19 cases: Relationship in two databases. *Journal of Public Health, 43*(2), 225-227. https://doi.org/10.1093/pubmed/fdaa212

Nguyen, T. D., Criss, S., Michaels, E. K., Cross, R. I., Michaels, J. S., Dwivedi, P., Huang, D., Hsu, E., Mukhija, K., Nguyen, L. H., Yardi, I., Allen, A. M., Acevedo-Garcia, D., & Gee, G. C. (2021). Progress and push-back: How the killings of Ahmaud Arbery, Breonna Taylor, and George Floyd impacted public discourse on race and racism on Twitter. *SSM-Population Health, 15*, 100922. https://doi.org/10.1016/j.ssmph.2021.100922

O'Flaherty, B. (2022). Why it won't ever be 2019 again: Guessing how COVID will change homelessness. *European Journal of Homelessness, 16*(1), 13-27.

Onwuachi-Willig, A. (2021). The trauma of awakening to racism: Did the tragic killing of George Floyd result in cultural trauma for whites? *Houston Law Review, 58*(4), 22269.

Patra, S. (2021). COVID-19: An opportunity to learn resilience from the elderly. *Journal of Geriatric Care and Research, 8*(1), 8-10.

Pinquart, M., & Sörensen, S. (2006). Gender differences in caregiver stressors, social resources, and health: An updated meta-analysis. *The Journals of Gerontology Series B: Psychological Sciences and Social Sciences, 61*(1), P33-P45. https://doi.org/10.1093/geronb/61.1.P33

Quadros, S., Garg, S., Ranjan, R., Vijayasarathi, G., & Mamun, M. A. (2021). Fear of COVID 19 infection across different cohorts: A scoping review. *Frontiers in Psychiatry, 12*, 708430. doi: 10.3389/fpsyt.2021.708430

Radcliffe, S. (2020, September 3). 60% of Americans have an underlying condition that increases COVID-19 risk. *Healthline.* https://www.healthline.com/health-news/60-percent-of-americans-have-underlying-condition-that-increases-covid19-risk

Ring, M., & Schuetz, J. (2021, August 9). Homelessness fell across most metro areas after the Great Recession. Will COVID-19 change that? *Brookings.* https://www.brookings.edu/research/homelessness-fell-across-most-metro-areas-after-the-great-recession-will-covid-19-change-that/

Schmidt, K. (2020, September 22). How many Americans are working from home? Not as many as you may think. *Grow.* https://grow.acorns.com/whos-working-from-home-charts/

Schulz, R., Visintainer, P., & Williamson, G. M. (1990). Psychiatric and physical morbidity effects of caregiving. *Journal of Gerontology, 45*(5), P181-P191. https://doi.org/10.1093/geronj/45.5.P181

Sharma, N., Chakrabarti, S., & Grover, S. (2016). Gender differences in caregiving among family-caregivers of people with mental illnesses. *World Journal of Psychiatry, 6*(1), 7- https://doi.org /17. 10.5498/wjp.v6.i1.7

Simon, M. (2020, August 5). Your income predicts how well you can socially distance. *Wired.* https://www.wired.com/story/your-income-predicts-how-well-you-can-socially-distance/

Sinclair, S., & Starck, J. G. (2021). George Floyd's death affected Black and White families differently. *Proceedings of the National Academy of Sciences, 118*(48). https://doi.org/10.1073/pnas.2115351118

Smith, A., Wright, H. F., Griffin, B. J., Ehman, A. C., Shoji, K., Love, T. M., Morrow, E., Locke, A., Call, M. E., Kerig, P. K., Olff, M., Benight, C. C., & Langenecker, S. A. (2021). Mental health risks differentially associated with immunocompromised status among healthcare workers and family members at the pandemic outset. *Brain, Behavior, & Immunity-Health, 15*, 100285. https:// doi.org/10.1016/j.bbih.2021.100285

Staub, E. (2003). *The psychology of good and evil: Why children, adults, and groups help and harm others.* Cambridge University Press.

Stefanova, V., Farrell, L., & Latu, I. (2021). Gender and the pandemic: Associations between caregiving, working from home, personal and career outcomes for women and men. *Current Psychology,* 1-17. https://doi.org/10.1007/s12144-021-02630-6

Stevenson, B. (2021, September 29). Women, work, and families: Recovering from the pandemic-induced recession. *Brookings.* https://www.brookings.edu/research/women-work-and-families-recovering-from-the-pandemic-induced-recession/

Sue, S., & Dhindsa, M. K. (2006). Ethnic and racial health disparities research: Issues and problems. *Health Education & Behavior, 33*(4), 459-469. https://doi.org/10.1177/1090198106287922

Swinkels, J., Tilburg, T. V., Verbakel, E., & Broese van Groenou, M. (2019). Explaining the gender gap in the caregiving burden of partner caregivers. *The Journals of Gerontology: Series B, 74*(2), 309-317. https://doi.org/10.1093/geronb/gbx036

van Kessel, S. A., Olde Hartman, T. C., Lucassen, P. L., & van Jaarsveld, C. H. (2022). Post-acute and long-COVID-19 symptoms in patients with mild diseases: A systematic review. *Family Practice, 39*(1), 159-167. https://doi.org/10.1093/fampra/cmab076

Verma, R., Kilgour, H. M., & Haase, K. R. (2022). The psychosocial impact of COVID-19 on older adults with cancer: A rapid review. *Current Oncology, 29*(2), 589-601. https://doi.org/10.3390/curroncol29020053

Wang, C., Cheong, Y., Zhu, Q., Havewala, M., & Ye, Y. (2022). Parent work–life conflict and adolescent adjustment during COVID-19: Mental health and parenting as mediators. *Journal of Family Psychology*. Advance online publication. https://doi.org/10.1037/fam0000948

Weiner, R. (2020, June 11). Political and health leaders' embrace of Floyd protests fuels debate over coronavirus restrictions. *The Washington Post*. https://www. washingtonpost.com/health/political-and-health-leaders-embrace-of-floyd -protests-fuels-debate-over-coronavirus-restrictions/2020/06/11/9c60bca6-a761-11ea-bb20-ebf0921f3bbd_story.html

Williams, D. R., & Sternthal, M. (2010). Understanding racial-ethnic disparities in health: Sociological contributions. *Journal of Health and Social Behavior, 51*(1_suppl), S15-S27. https://doi.org/10.1177/00221465103838

Yadav, U. N., Yadav, O. P., Singh, D., Ghimire, S., Rayamajhee, B., Mistry, S. K., Rawal, L. B., Ali, A. R. M. M., Tamang, M. K., & Mehta, S. L. (2021). Perceived fear of COVID-19 and its associated factors among Nepalese older adults in eastern Nepal: A cross-sectional study. *PLOS ONE, 16*(7), e0254825. https:// doi.org/10.1371/journal.pone.0254825

Yearby, R. (2020). Structural racism and health disparities: Reconfiguring the social determinants of health framework to include the root cause. *The Journal of Law, Medicine & Ethics, 48*(3), 518-526. https://doi.org/10.1177/10 73110520958876

The Psychology of Good and Evil in the Covid-19 Pandemic

The broad issue of why people show good or evil behavior is arguably a deep philosophical question that has vexed many, including psychologists, who have fundamentally tried to understand both constructs as a complex consequence of personal, social, and societal factors (e.g., Staub, 2003; Miller, 2004). While this chapter includes some discussion of prosocial behavior displayed during the pandemic, tragically, much of the pandemic will be—or should be—remembered for the many destructive and antisocial acts of behavior occurring or emanating from it. As such, this chapter aims to place these acts in some proper context by exploring phenomena particularly from the social psychological literature as well as some select historical comparisons.

(Toward An Attempt of) The Good: Helping Others and Staying Home

Healthcare professionals, in particular, have often been embraced and celebrated as "heroes" who were at "war" with the coronavirus; curiously, though, many of these frontline providers have rejected such labels (e.g., Pennella & Ragonese, 2020). Critics of the hero label argued that it limits discussion of what the boundaries of the duty to treat others entail (Cox, 2020) while also removing appropriate policy decisions away from politicians and onto the workers themselves (Halberg et al., 2021).

Indeed, in my original analysis of the initial state of the pandemic from mid-March to mid-April 2020 (Miller, 2020), I discussed the appalling state that many healthcare workers found themselves in by not having enough personal protective equipment (PPE) and being forced to wear garbage bags as a form of protection. Thankfully, those supplies became increasingly available to medical staff though—as early as July 2020—Dr. Peter Hotez, the dean of tropical medicine at Baylor College of Medicine, was declaring that America:

> …[was approaching] one of the most unstable times in the history of our country. We will have hospitals overwhelmed and not only in terms of ICU beds and hospitals—and that's bad—but exhausted hospital staff and hospital staff that's getting ill themselves (Holcombe, 2020, p. 1).

Related to this previous point, there is an awful irony that so many individuals failed to heed the pleas of these "hero" frontline medical providers by not following recommended safety guidelines during the pandemic, such as staying home. Consider the following plea from one physician in regards to her recommendation of how to spend Thanksgiving in 2020 (which was right before the expected 2020-2021 winter Covid surge):

> The only responsible way to spend Thanksgiving this year is in your home or with people you have been living with for the past two weeks...We are all tired, and longing for comfort and joy. But now, with a vaccine coming, there is an end in sight. It will not be long before we can embrace one another, eat together and let this year become a distant memory. I beg of you, don't let this Thanksgiving be your last (Poorman, 2020, pp. 3-4).

The pleas of physicians like Dr. Poorman notwithstanding, it is difficult to tease apart, in an absolute sense, how much of one's adherence to prudent health protocols is exclusively due to personal versus social or societal factors. However, regarding the latter, there is evidence that American States with political leaders and policies that stressed mask-wearing and prolonging stay-at-home orders, tended to fair better in their Covid case counts as of summer 2020 (Yan, 2020). And yet, Sheth and Wright (2020) found evidence that altruism was not a predictive factor of compliance to stay at home and social distancing requirements among college students. However, Rieger (2020) found that an altruistic appeal designed to convince college students to get vaccinated so that such an act could potentially reduce risk to others was a particularly potent persuasion strategy. Classic work from the social psychologists Latané and Darley (1970) has long held that helping behavior is, by no means, the default reaction from others as there are four decisions we entertain before we decide to consider the fifth step of whether to actually provide help. In short, if we do not personally believe a situation is an emergency in need of attention or we do not believe there is a reason to personally act, then we are not likely to engage in altruistic behavior. This perspective might offer even greater insight into some reasons why individuals have flagrantly not done anything in the pandemic to amend their behavior as noted in the next section.

The Bad: Indifference to the Virus

Even if individuals weren't actively or purposefully striving to show indifferent reactions to the virus, noted epidemiologist Tara C. Smith (2020) put it quite bluntly in July 2020—which was, of course, just a few months into the pandemic and well before the availability of vaccines—that "You might be tired of living this way, but the virus doesn't care" (p. 3) and added that "...it's still our collective behavior that determines the trajectory of this epidemic" (p. 4). Dr. Deborah Birx, the leading Trump White House coronavirus response coordinator suggested in late March 2020 that in a "best case scenario" there would likely be 100,000 to 200,000 American deaths but if nothing were done then upwards of two million Americans were likely to die in the then-burgeoning pandemic (Kesslen, 2020). Perhaps no official government or scientific officials wanted to suggest or believe it at the time, but it was foolhardy to have even presumed that there would be some "perfect" model of appropriate social and health behavior displayed by others given what we know about human nature. Perhaps it was an unfair criticism (to some degree) to have suggested that America had effectively given up on the pandemic by often flagrantly ignoring health advice aimed at slowing the spread of the virus (Madrigal & Meyer, 2020). Yet, during the pandemic, there have been endless images of individuals and groups who were seemingly not just oblivious, or indifferent to the notion of modifying their behavior in any meaningful way whatsoever—but almost downright hostile to it. For instance, a bar resort in the Lake of the Ozarks, Missouri, received much notoriety in both the summer of 2020 and 2021 for its overt overcrowding, lack of mask-wearing, and (once it was available) shunning of the vaccine despite the fact that this area of the country was particularly hard hit in the Delta wave (Korecki, 2021). Though outdoor sports venues were largely welcoming back fans in spring 2021, a near-capacity crowd of 40,000 individuals at the Texas Rangers' Globe Life Field baseball stadium on Opening Day in early April 2021 was widely criticized, particularly since less than a third of Americans had been vaccinated by that point (Al-Khateeb, 2021). Perhaps not surprisingly, those who remained unvaccinated were also less likely to wear a mask (Hoonhout, 2021). As a testament to the relative predictability to the nature of the virus influenced by human behavior, Covid cases tended to sharply rise after holiday events (which commonly featured social gatherings) from the earliest weeks of the pandemic starting with the 2020 Memorial Day holiday (Pell et al., 2020).

Political ideology clearly played an important determinant of individual and collective actions regarding the virus. For instance, from the earliest months of the pandemic, Democrats have been far more likely to endorse always wearing masks in public than Republicans (e.g., Edwards-Levy, 2020) and were much less comfortable to returning to their pre-pandemic routines (Agiesta, 2020). Culture and situational factors also influenced many of these decisions. For instance, there is much evidence that the pandemic may have amplified one's initial views about related policies and health practices through group polarization processes (e.g., Bernacer et al., 2021). Yet, even from the earliest months of the pandemic, there was a widespread sense that mandating how one should behave was a threat to one's personal sense of freedom (Andrew, 2020). Indeed, the pandemic has at least questioned whether health concerns should prevail over real or perceived democratic liberties (France 24, 2022). In a similar vein, not surprisingly, the more individualistic (as opposed to collectivistic) a country was—such as the United States—the more Covid cases and related mortalities it had (Maaravi et al., 2021). There is also evidence that individuals simply may have become desensitized to its effects over time. Stevens et al. (2021) found that the level of anxiety present and reacted to in online Tweets declined as the pandemic progressed with the suggestion that individuals may have become more nonchalant regarding the threats and suffering associated with the virus. Lwin and colleagues (2020) also found that anxiety-laden Tweets declined from late January to early April 2020 but was replaced with more anger and indignation particularly with respect to stay-at-home orders.

Personality and individual differences clearly were important determinants of adaptive and maladaptive behavior during the pandemic. For instance, not surprisingly, Aschwanden et al. (2020) found that neuroticism was associated with greater concerns about the pandemic, but conscientiousness was correlated with greater precautions; by contrast, extraversion was related to shorter duration estimates of the pandemic. Nowak and colleagues (2020) found that the Dark Triad traits of psychopathy, Machiavellianism, and narcissism were less associated with preventative measures and more dysfunctional reactions like hoarding. While these aforementioned traits (along with low agreeableness) are indeed important determinants of compliance with governmental and health restrictions, how the pandemic was perceived may have been particularly critical given the powerful nature of this situation (Zajenkowski et al., 2020). In addition to political ideology, perceptions of mask-wearing (e.g., whether or not they are "cool") impacted such behavior as well—and men were more likely than women to endorse such views (Capraro & Barcelo, 2020); arguably, perceptions of following masculine appropriate roles might have influenced these gender differences amongst men who may have felt a particular need to exert individuality and be more hesitant to show healthful behavior (Wong, 2020).

But why wouldn't people universally just acknowledge the potential gravity of the virus—for themselves or others? The health belief model has long been an influential guide as to why, when, and whether one is likely to take preventative action in the face of health threat—or frankly, whether one perceives a health threat at all (Rosenstock, 1974). In brief, this model suggests that a host of demographic and psychological variables and knowledge about a disease collectively lead one to perceive its seriousness and susceptibility to it; these factors (along with cues to action, such as reminders from others) cause us to assess and weigh both perceived benefits to action minus the barriers to action and the perceived threat of the illness itself. To provide one such example of how this model has been used to understand pandemic-related health decisions, Zampetakis and Melas (2021) explored why someone would (or would not) choose to receive the Covid vaccine once it was available. Among their chief findings, these researchers found that individuals were particularly likely to seek the vaccine if they realized the potential risk of getting the virus (by remaining unvaccinated) along with a relatively low risk associated with the ill effects of receiving the vaccine itself.

Prominent social psychologists Elliot Aronson and Carol Tavris (2020) considered the larger question of why one might have simply dismissed the virus or pandemic as a non-consequential event for their health or lives—their answer was cognitive dissonance, which is the well-known phenomenon first documented by Leon Festinger (1957) to show how we often change our behavior to match our attitudes when they are inconsistent with each other. For instance, Aronson and Tavris (2020) discussed how smokers often dismiss the concerning potential health effects of that by uttering statements like how it keeps them thin; in a similar sense, they contend that people needed to justify to themselves their actions for not taking the pandemic seriously, so they made such proclamations that masks were uncomfortable or one was fighting for their constitutional rights and freedoms. People may have also simply denied or rationalized away the potential ill effects of the virus especially if others (whether they be in person or online) reinforced those views through a confirmation bias-like process (Marples, 2020).

Dr. Anthony Fauci suggested that another important attitude to factor into this analysis was an anti-science bias where individuals either did not trust or understand scientific details or those who relayed such information (Slisco, 2020). In examining Tweets collected between January and May 2020, Rao and colleagues (2021) found that Covid cases tended to correlate with the proportion of anti-science conservatives. Interestingly though, Sanchez and Dunning (2021) conducted three related studies which found that political ideology was not clearly associated with anti-science beliefs but rather whether one had a more general positive assessment of scientists.

To place some of these questionable behaviors in some historical context, individuals have also previously reacted with a sense of indifference or even indignation in the wake of new health threats or mandates as evidenced by two different events from the 1980s. Just as important as mask-wearing has been in fighting the Covid pandemic, it became increasingly clear that condom-wearing was critical to prevent HIV infections—yet, many chose not to heed such warnings often to their grave detriment (Hedden, 2020). Further, when New York became the first U.S. State to mandate seatbelt wearing while driving, there were widespread calls against governmental influence over personal freedoms (Hauser, 2020). In short, well before the coronavirus pandemic, there has been a long history of conflict between government restrictions and initiatives in the name of public health versus a perception that personal liberties were thusly being thwarted by such actions (e.g., Harris, 2021).

The Ugly: Racism, Violence, Nationalism, and Hate

Anyone remotely familiar with the field of psychology knows the full spectrum of human behavior—which includes destructive and vicious acts. Humans have a tendency to attribute "bad" actions to only "bad" actors—a process that social psychologists have typically referred to as the fundamental attribution error or correspondence bias (e.g., Gilbert & Malone, 1995). Indeed, there are plenty of examples of individuals that would likely widely be viewed as having nefarious motives carrying out inhospitable acts—such as ISIS terrorists (among others) selling fake PPE online (not just for personal profit but) to finance terrorism (Herridge, 2020).

As discussed elsewhere in this book, during the pandemic there have been many shocking acts of racism and hate often laced with violence related to trajectories of nationalist themes (Bieber, 2022). In addition to threats against school board commissioners, select politicians and public health officials, many lawmakers have tried to spread misinformation about the pandemic and the vaccine (Smyth & Bohrer, 2021). Others, including some with medical backgrounds, have also spread falsehoods to governmental bodies with the general intention of eliminating Covid restrictions or face mask or vaccine mandates (Salcedo, 2021).

Individuals have advanced mistruths and even conspiracies about select events well before the pandemic. Arguably though, it is one matter to debate over, for instance, whether Lee Harvey Oswald acted alone in the assassination of President John F. Kennedy versus endorsing beliefs that undermine and threaten larger public health measures. Eberl et al. (2021) offer evidence that those who endorse such outlandish ideas that, for example, Bill Gates or 5G cell signals were behind the pandemic—or, more sinisterly, the so-called "plandemic"— were also more likely to endorse populist attitudes independent of political ideology. Suthaharan and colleagues (2021) bolster the point that political ideology alone does not necessarily predict Covid-related conspiratorial thinking; in particular, they found that paranoia was more associated with fringe QAnon conspiracy theories. Drinkwater et al. (2021) further add that such thinking becomes attractive to those who may doubt or deny official narratives of an event, like many of the themes advanced by Donald Trump (e.g., Tollefson, 2021). QAnon also provided a means to reject public health messaging. Originating as an anonymous online message board post in 2017, QAnon is a group of conspiracy theorists striving to overthrow the "deep state" and bring about rapture; there is growing concern that this group may attempt to engage in more severe domestic terrorist attacks to achieve its stated aims and increase its popularity (Hodwitz et al., 2022). Indeed, the QAnon movement was widely supportive of the 2021 U. S. Capitol attacks (Armaly et al., 2022) and is also related to Christian nationalism which, in turn, has been viewed as a threat to American democracy (Gorski & Perry, 2022).

Anti-Semitism has also been displayed during the pandemic with varying degrees of subtleness. Some of these expressions have been rather overt such as at an anti-vaccine protest in Glogow, Poland where throngs of individuals shouted that Jews were behind the "plandemic" (Zaig, 2021). Anti-Defamation League CEO Jonathan A. Greenblatt (2021) reported 2,204 anti-Semitic acts in America in 2020 which was 10% higher than the previous year and one of the highest of the prior five years. He further added: "…because antisemitism so often has been the canary in the coal mine of hatred, the historic high of antisemitic incidents of the past several years should alarm far more than Jewish people" (p. 10). Many of these acts not just featured conspiracy-related themes, such as the aforementioned ones, but also purposeful online acts of hate like "Zoombombing" (where online meetings, such as Zoom, were disrupted with egregious hateful speech). Zoombombing appreciably increased following the start of the pandemic; while many such acts could be described as online disruptions or pranks, one study found that 86% of compiled YouTube clips of "Zoombombing" featured racist, misogynist, homophobic, or other toxic content (Elmer et al., 2021).

One of the more disturbing trends often affiliated with both anti-Semitism and Covid-conspiratorial thinking—and even broader anti-vaccination or anti-mitigation policies—has been the perverse way by which the Holocaust has been invoked to support such ideology. Individuals (often those protesting against various health mandates) and select politicians alike have tried to somehow link governmental mandates to the actions taken against the Jews in Nazi Europe (Bandler, 2021). Some of these protesters even constructed yellow Stars of David with the word "unvaccinated" to somehow equate their plight to the 6 million murdered Jews. Not only is such messaging a grossly inaccurate historical comparison, but it remains in an egregious assault on victims of the Holocaust as well.

Political leaders and public officials have a considerable means to potentially shape or sway significant portions of public opinion about various issues. The aforementioned article (Bandler, 2021) also detailed how many prominent politicians have similarly convoluted Holocaust themes for their own political motives related to the pandemic. As president during the first several months of the pandemic, Donald Trump was accused of making many racially charged statements with anti-Asian overtones, such as his frequent invocation of Covid as "kung flu" (Oprysko, 2020) or his perceived racist or sexist retort to a female Asian-American reporter to "ask China" in regards to her question about challenges associated with Covid testing (Darcy, 2020). To offer another historical contrast, while Ronald Reagan was not known to publicly and explicitly disparage homosexuals during the initial surge of the AIDS crisis, he did not even mention the disease until four years after it was first discovered in 1981; however, his Press Secretary, Larry Speakes, made comments now widely viewed as homophobic during press conferences (Lawson, 2015).

As influential as presidents and public officials can be in helping to shape public opinion, social psychologists have long known that there are a myriad of factors that can lead individuals to act in hateful or destructive ways. Consistent with the concern that I discussed in my previous analysis (Miller, 2020), hate crimes increased from 2020 to 2021 in the United States—but it was particularly pronounced with respect to anti-Asian hate (which saw a 73% increase in 2020, according to FBI statistics; Venkatraman, 2021). Tragically, the pandemic has brought much racist stigmatization to the larger Asian community worldwide (Ng, 2020).

Unfortunately, the pandemic has uniquely allowed for a toxic stew of varying social psychological principles that helped to illuminate some of the possible reasons behind these destructive behaviors. For instance, perceived threats have often been associated with increased adherence or acceptance of authoritarianism—and, indeed, Hartman and colleagues (2021) found evidence of this connection in the pandemic, particularly as it pertained to anti-immigration sentiment. Terror management theory has highlighted how we fear death and in order to try to deny it we may ultimately show prejudicial attitudes towards those perceived as outsiders; naturally, the pandemic provided a powerful means of highlighting this fear and, with it, some of its concerning behavioral effects (Pyszczynski et al., 2021).

Given earlier psychological research that masks can promote deindividuation (e.g., Miller & Rowold, 1979), at the start of the pandemic, there was some concern that face masks might widely facilitate crime (e.g., Sheard & Farrell, 2020). Despite some high-profile cases that face masks and related protective gear may have aided suspects in carrying out crimes—like the unknown individual who allegedly placed explosives outside the Republican and Democratic National Committee buildings the night before the January 6, 2021 Capitol riots (Balsamo, 2022)—this does not seem to have occurred on a widespread level. On a promising note, there is evidence that face masks do not seem to dehumanize individuals (Utych, 2021) and they may even allow us to be more spontaneous in our social reactions (Perini & Sciara, 2022). However, face masks may also confuse our ability to read emotions (Carbon, 2020) and promote psychological distance (Fatfouta & Trope, 2022).

Lepore (2021) offered a provocative analysis where she entertains a common sentiment that society almost feels like it is coming apart given widely perceived societal divisions, social disconnections (perhaps exacerbated, ironically, with online social media), and a common sense that government and other societal structures have been dysfunctional. While she does argue that governments cannot neglect its "obligations of care," she keenly notes that:

> Forging stronger bonds in a post-pandemic world, if one ever comes, will require acts of moral imagination that are not part of any political ideology or corporate mission statement, but are, instead, functions of the human condition: tenderness, compassion, longing, generosity, allegiance and affection. These, too, are the only real answers to loneliness, alienation, dislocation and disintegration (p. 17).

In reflecting on most of the psychological phenomena considered in this chapter, as a prolonged stressful and threatening event, the pandemic has clearly served as a breeding ground for highly noxious behavior. What remains unknown is how these effects will not just shape behavior in the long-run (both individually and collectively) but also how will future generations come to understand why so much indifference (at best) and hate was displayed during the pandemic rather than larger consistent focus on the common societal good.

References

Agiesta, J. (2020, June 10). CNN poll: Public split on return to routine due to coronavirus. *CNN.* https://www.cnn.com/2020/06/10/politics/cnn-poll-coronavirus/index.html

Al-Khateeb, Z. (2021, April 5). Video shows fans packed into Rangers' Globe Life Field for home opener: 'Selfish and dumb'. *The Sporting News.* https://www.sportingnews.com/us/mlb/news/video-shows-fans-packed-into-rangers-globe-life-field/8mrl8r0yfrvm1xqvjy8cxsjbh

Andrew, S. (2020, May 6). The psychology behind why some people won't wear masks. *CNN.* https://www.cnn.com/2020/05/06/health/why-people-dont-wear-masks-wellness-trnd/index.html

Armaly, M. T., Buckley, D. T., & Enders, A. M. (2022). Christian nationalism and political violence: Victimhood, racial identity, conspiracy, and support for the capitol attacks. *Political Behavior, 44*(2), 937-960. https://doi.org/10.1007/s11109-021-09758-y

Aronson, E., & Tavris, C. (2020, July 12). The role of cognitive dissonance in the pandemic. *The Atlantic.* https://www.theatlantic.com/ideas/archive/2020/07/role-cognitive-dissonance-pandemic/614074/

Aschwanden, D., Strickhouser, J. E., Sesker, A. A., Lee, J. H., Luchetti, M., Stephan, Y., Sutin, A. R., & Terracciano, A. (2021). Psychological and behavioural responses to coronavirus disease 2019: The role of personality. *European Journal of Personality, 35*(1), 51-66. https://doi.org/10.1002/per.2281

Balsamo, M. (2022, January 5). A year after Jan. 6, FBI still hunting for pipe bomber and other insurrection suspects. *PBS.* https://www.pbs.org/newshour/nation/a-year-after-jan-6-fbi-still-hunting-for-pipe-bomber-and-other-insurrection-suspects

Bandler, K. (2021, December 26/28). Normalization of Holocaust parallels in COVID era. *The Jerusalem Post.* https://www.jpost.com/opinion/article-689829

Bernacer, J., García-Manglano, J., Camina, E., & Güell, F. (2021). Polarization of beliefs as a consequence of the COVID-19 pandemic: The case of Spain. *PLOS ONE, 16*(7), e0254511. https://doi.org/10.1371/journal.pone.0254511

Bieber, F. (2022). Global nationalism in times of the COVID-19 pandemic. *Nationalities Papers, 50*(1), 13-25. https://doi.org/10.1017/nps.2020.35

Capraro, V., & Barcelo, H. (2020). The effect of messaging and gender on intentions to wear a face covering to slow down COVID-19 transmission. *arXiv preprint arXiv:2005.05467.*

Carbon, C. C. (2020). Wearing face masks strongly confuses counterparts in reading emotions. *Frontiers in Psychology, 11,* 566886. https://doi.org/10.3389/fpsyg.2020.566886

Cox, C. L. (2020). 'Healthcare Heroes': Problems with media focus on heroism from healthcare workers during the COVID-19 pandemic. *Journal of Medical Ethics, 46*(8), 510-513. http://dx.doi.org/10.1136/medethics-2020-106398

Darcy, O. (2020, May 12). Trump abruptly ends press conference after contentious exchange with reporters. *CNN.* https://www.cnn.com/2020/05/11/media/trump-press-briefing-weijia-jian-kaitlan-collins/index.html

Drinkwater, K. G., Dagnall, N., Denovan, A., & Walsh, R. S. (2021). To what extent have conspiracy theories undermined COVID-19: Strategic narratives? *Frontiers in Communication, 6,* 576198. https://doi.org/10.3389/fcomm.2021.576198

Eberl, J. M., Huber, R. A., & Greussing, E. (2021). From populism to the "plandemic": Why populists believe in COVID-19 conspiracies. *Journal of Elections, Public Opinion and Parties, 31*(sup1), 272-284. https://doi.org/10.1080/17457289.2021.1924730

Edwards-Levy, A. (2020, July 27). Wearing a mask is more popular — and a little less partisan — than you might expect. *HuffPost.* https://www.huffpost.com/entry/face-mask-poll-support-partisan_n_5f1cc69ac5b69fd4730d52be

Elmer, G., Neville, S. J., Burton, A., & Ward-Kimola, S. (2021). Zoombombing during a global pandemic. *Social Media+ Society, 7*(3), 1-12 https://doi.org/10.1177/20563051211035356

Fatfouta, R., & Trope, Y. (2022). Keeping one's distance: Mask wearing is implicitly associated with psychological distance. *Social Psychological and Personality Science, 13*(4), 875-883. https://doi.org/10.1177/1948550621104406

Festinger, L. (1957). *A theory of cognitive dissonance.* Stanford University Press.

France 24. (2022, January 6). Health first, freedom second? How Covid is changing democracies. *France24.* https://www.france24.com/en/live-news/20220106-health-first-freedom-second-how-covid-is-changing-democracies

Gilbert, D. T., & Malone, P. S. (1995). The correspondence bias. *Psychological Bulletin, 117*(1), 21–38. https://doi.org/10.1037/0033-2909.117.1.21

Gorski, P.S., & Perry, S. L. (2022). *The flag and the cross: White Christian nationalism and the threat to American democracy.* Oxford University Press.

Greenblatt, J. A. (2021, April 27). Covid quarantine didn't stop antisemitic attacks from rising to near-historic highs. *NBC News.* https://www.nbcnews.com/think/opinion/covid-quarantine-didn-t-stop-antisemitic-attacks-rising-near-historic-ncna1265425

Halberg, N., Jensen, P. S., & Larsen, T. S. (2021). We are not heroes—The flipside of the hero narrative amidst the COVID19 pandemic: A Danish hospital ethnography. *Journal of Advanced Nursing, 77*(5), 2429-2436. https://doi.org/10.1111/jan.14811

Harris, C. E. (2021). The conflict of public health law and civil liberties: The role of research data and First Amendment law. *The American Journal of Medicine, 134*(11), 1312-1313. https://doi.org/10.1016/j.amjmed.2021.04.038

Hartman, T. K., Stocks, T. V. A., McKay, R., Martin, J., Levita, L., Martinez, A. P., Mason, L., McBride, O., Murphy, J., Shevlin, M., Bennett, K. M., Hyland, P., Karatzias, T., Vallières, F., & Bentall, R. P. (2021). The authoritarian dynamic during the COVID-19 pandemic: Effects on nationalism and anti-immigrant sentiment. *Social Psychological and Personality Science, 12*(7), 1274-1285. https://doi.org/10.1177/1948550620978023

Hauser, C. (2020, October 15/16). In fights over face masks, echoes of the American seatbelt wars. *The New York Times.* https://www.nytimes.com/2020/10/15/us/seatbelt-laws-history-masks-covid.html

Hedden, T. (2020, July 25). Masks stop coronavirus. Getting AIDS showed me the stupidity of not wearing them. *NBC News.* https://www.nbcnews.com/think/opinion/masks-stop-coronavirus-getting-aids-showed-me-stupidity-not-wearing-ncna1234878

Herridge, C. (2020, August 13). ISIS accused of selling fake PPE online to finance terrorism. *CBS News.* https://www.cbsnews.com/news/isis-accused-of-selling-fake-ppe-online-to-finance-terrorism/

Hodwitz, O., King, S., & Thompson, J. (2022). QAnon: The calm before the storm. *Society,* 1-12. https://doi.org/10.1007/s12115-022-00688-x

Holcombe, M. (2020, July 11). Expert warns the US is approaching 'one of the most unstable times in the history of our country'. *CNN.* https://www.cnn.com/2020/07/11/health/us-coronavirus-saturday/index.html

Hoonhout, T. (2021, April 9). Poll: Unvaccinated Americans significantly more likely to not wear mask. *National Review.* https://www.nationalreview.com/news/poll-unvaccinated-americans-significantly-more-likely-to-not-wear-mask/

Kesslen, B. (2020, March 30). Dr. Birx predicts up to 200,000 U.S. coronavirus deaths 'if we do things almost perfectly'. *NBC News.* https://www.nbcnews.com/news/us-news/dr-deborah-birx-predicts-200-000-deaths-if-we-do-n1171876

Korecki, N. (2021, July 27). 'What's Covid?' Why people at America's hardest-partying lake are not about to get vaccinated. *Politico.* https://www.politico.com/news/magazine/2021/07/27/ozarks-lake-covid-unvaccinated-500784

Lawson, R. (2015, December 1). The Reagan administration's unearthed response to the AIDS crisis is chilling. *Vanity Fair.* https://www.vanityfair.com/news/2015/11/reagan-administration-response-to-aids-crisis

Latané, B., & Darley, J. (1970). *The unresponsive bystander: Why doesn't he help?* Prentice Hall.

Lepore, J. (2021, November 25). Is society coming apart? *The Guardian.* https://www.theguardian.com/society/2021/nov/25/society-thatcher-reagan-covid-pandemic

Lwin, M. O., Lu, J., Sheldenkar, A., Schulz, P. J., Shin, W., Gupta, R., & Yang, Y. (2020). Global sentiments surrounding the COVID-19 pandemic on Twitter: Analysis of Twitter trends. *JMIR Public Health and Surveillance, 6*(2), e19447. https://doi.org/10.2196/19447

Maaravi, Y., Levy, A., Gur, T., Confino, D., & Segal, S. (2021). "The tragedy of the commons": How individualism and collectivism affected the spread of the COVID-19 pandemic. *Frontiers in Public Health, 9,* 627559. https://doi.org/10.3389/fpubh.2021.627559

Madrigal, A. C., & Meyer, R. (2020, June 7). America is giving up on the pandemic. *The Atlantic.* https://www.theatlantic.com/science/archive/2020/06/america-giving-up-on-pandemic/612796/

Marples, S. (2020, August 16). Pandemic denial: Why some people can't accept Covid-19's realities. *CNN.* https://www.cnn.com/2020/08/16/health/pandemic-covid-19-denial-mental-health-wellness/index.html

Miller, A.G. (Ed.). (2004). *The social psychology of good and evil.* Guilford.

Miller, E. D. (2020). The COVID-19 pandemic crisis: The loss and trauma event of our time. *Journal of Loss and Trauma, 25*(6-7), 560-572. https://doi.org/10.1080/15325024.2020.1759217

Miller, F. G., & Rowold, K. L. (1979). Halloween masks and deindividuation. *Psychological Reports, 44*(2), 422. https://doi.org/10.2466/pr0.1979.44.2.422

Ng, E. (2020). The pandemic of hate is giving COVID-19 a helping hand. *The American Journal of Tropical Medicine and Hygiene, 102*(6), 1158-1159. https://doi.org/10.4269/ajtmh.20-0285

Nowak, B., Brzóska, P., Piotrowski, J., Sedikides, C., Żemojtel-Piotrowska, M., & Jonason, P. K. (2020). Adaptive and maladaptive behavior during the COVID-19 pandemic: The roles of Dark Triad traits, collective narcissism, and health beliefs. *Personality and Individual Differences, 167,* 110232. https://doi.org/10.1016/j.paid.2020.110232

Oprysko, (2020, June 22). McEnany defends Trump's 'kung flu' comment at rally. *Politico.* https://www.politico.com/news/2020/06/22/mcenany-defends-trump-kung-flu-comment-333814

Pell, S., Buckner, C., & Dupree, J. (2020, June 9). Coronavirus hospitalizations rise sharply in several states following Memorial Day. *The Washington Post.* https://www.washingtonpost.com/health/2020/06/09/coronavirus-hospitalizations-rising/

Pennella, A. R., & Ragonese, A. (2020). Health professionals and COVID-19 pandemic: Heroes in a new war. *Journal of Health and Social Sciences, 5*(2), 169-176.

Perini, M., & Sciara, S. (2022). Wearing an anti-COVID face mask predisposes to spontaneity and ideas' expression in social interactions: Findings from a pilot experiment. *Trends in Psychology.* https://doi.org/10.1007/s43076-021-00139-2

Poorman, E. (2020, November 19). A Doctor's Thanksgiving plea: Stay home and stay safe. *NPR.* https://www.npr.org/sections/health-shots/2020/11/19/936243397/a-doctors-thanksgiving-plea-stay-home-and-stay-safe

Pyszczynski, T., Lockett, M., Greenberg, J., & Solomon, S. (2021). Terror management theory and the COVID-19 pandemic. *Journal of Humanistic Psychology, 61*(2), 173-189. https://doi.org/10.1177/0022167820959488

Rao, A., Morstatter, F., Hu, M., Chen, E., Burghardt, K., Ferrara, E., & Lerman, K. (2021). Political partisanship and antiscience attitudes in online discussions about COVID-19: Twitter content analysis. *Journal of Medical Internet Research, 23*(6), e26692. https://doi.org/10.2196/26692

Rieger, M. O. (2020). Triggering altruism increases the willingness to get vaccinated against COVID-19. *Social Health and Behavior, 3*(3), 78-82. https://doi.org/10.4103/SHB.SHB_39_20

Rosenstock, I. M. (1974). Historical origins of the health belief model. *Health Education Monographs, 2*(4), 328-335. https://doi.org/10.1177/109019817400200403

Salcedo, A. (2021, June 9). A doctor falsely told lawmakers vaccines magnetize people: 'They can put a key on their forehead. It sticks.' *The Washington Post.* https://www.washingtonpost.com/nation/2021/06/09/sherri-tenpenny-magnetized-vaccine-ohio/

Sanchez, C., & Dunning, D. (2021). The anti-scientists bias: The role of feelings about scientists in COVID-19 attitudes and behaviors. *Journal of Applied Social Psychology, 51*(4), 461-473. https://doi.org/10.1111/jasp.12748

Sheard, E., & Farrell, G. (2020). COVID facemasks as crime facilitators. *Journal of Scandinavian Studies in Criminology and Crime Prevention, 2*, 171-190.

Sheth, K., & Wright, G. C. (2020). The usual suspects: Do risk tolerance, altruism, and health predict the response to COVID-19? *Review of Economics of the Household, 18*(4), 1041-1052. https://doi.org/10.1007/s11150-020-09515-w

Slisco, A. (2020, June 18). Fauci blames 'anti-science bias' for people not following COVID-19 rules. *Newsweek.* https://www.newsweek.com/fauci-blames-anti-science-bias-people-not-following-covid-19-rules-1512019

Smith, T. C. (2020, July 22). The pandemic isn't over. We need to act accordingly. *Self.* https://www.self.com/story/coronavirus-pandemic-isnt-over

Smyth, J.C., & Bohrer, B. (2021, February 28). Some GOP state lawmakers help spread COVID-19 misinformation. *AP News.* https://apnews.com/article/legislature-ohio-misinformation-coronavirus-pandemic-0c19a98d7dd4f745cfa935d6602528aa

Staub, E. (2003). *The psychology of good and evil: Children, adults and groups helping and harming others.* Cambridge University Press.

Stevens, H. R., Oh, Y. J., & Taylor, L. D. (2021). Desensitization to fear-inducing COVID-19 health news on Twitter: Observational study. *JMIR Infodemiology, 1*(1), e26876. https://doi.org/ 10.2196/26876

Suthaharan, P., Reed, E., Leptourgos, P., Kenney, J., Uddenberg, S., Mathys, C., Litman, L., Robinson, J., Moss, A., Taylor, J. R., Groman, S. M., & Corlett, P. R. (2021). Paranoia and belief updating during the COVID-19 crisis. *Nature Human Behaviour, 5*(9), 1190-1202. https://doi.org/10.1038/s41562-021-01176-8

Tollefson, J. (2021). Tracking QAnon: How Trump turned conspiracy-theory research upside down. *Nature, 590*(7845), 192-193. https://doi.org/10.1038/d41586-021-00257-y

Utych, S. M. (2021). No, face masks aren't dehumanizing. *Political Studies Review, 19*(3), 528-535. https://doi.org/10.1177/1478929921993764

Venkatraman, S. (2021, October 25). Anti-Asian hate crimes rose 73% last year, updated FBI data says. *NBC News.* https://www.nbcnews.com/news/asian-america/anti-asian-hate-crimes-rose-73-last-year-updated-fbi-data-says-rcna3741

Wong, B. (2020, July 24). The psychology behind why men refuse to wear face masks. *HuffPost.* https://www.huffpost.com/entry/psychology-why-men-refuse-to-wear-masks_l_5f18a364c5b6296fbf3cf89d

Yan, H. (2020, July 22). 'From worst to first': These states have tamed coronavirus, even after reopening. Here's how they're doing it, and why they can't let up. *CNN.* https://www.cnn.com/2020/07/15/health/coronavirus-under-control-states/index.html

Zaij, G. (2021, July 21). 'Jews are behind the pandemic' chanted at anti-vaccine protest in Poland. *The Jerusalem Post.* https://www.jpost.com/diaspora/antisemitism/jews-are-behind-the-pandemic-chanted-at-anti-vaccine-protest-in-poland-674491

Zajenkowski, M., Jonason, P. K., Leniarska, M., & Kozakiewicz, Z. (2020). Who complies with the restrictions to reduce the spread of COVID-19?: Personality and perceptions of the COVID-19 situation. *Personality and Individual Differences, 166,* 110199. https://doi.org/10.1016/j.paid.2020.110199

Zampetakis, L. A., & Melas, C. (2021). The health belief model predicts vaccination intentions against COVID-19: A survey experiment approach. *Applied Psychology: Health and Well-Being, 13*(2), 469-484. https://doi.org/10.1111/aphw.12262

CHAPTER EIGHT

The Psychology of Place and Environment Post Covid-19

In the earliest days of the pandemic, much of the devastation of Covid was particularly pronounced in urban areas—especially New York City. As such, much of this chapter discusses some of the challenges of urban life and design in the aftermath of this crisis. However, some broader consideration of how the pandemic impacted our ability to navigate place and environment (and how select physical environments may have impacted us during the pandemic) will also be discussed.

A Select Consideration of How Life Changed During the Pandemic

In some respects, the pandemic was about the effects of simply staying home and finding fulfilment in mundane tasks that most individuals did not previously consider as particularly eventful on any regular basis. A survey conducted by OnePoll of 2,005 American adults during the pandemic found that incredibly 32% of the sample reported that doing the laundry was the event highlight of their week; this sample also found that over a third of respondents found some satisfaction in grocery shopping or filling their car gas tank and 69% endorsed the notion that any new experience felt thrilling given the amount of time spent indoors (Melore, 2021). However, it really would not be a fair characterization to suggest that most individuals were somehow captive and unable to go anywhere even at the height of stay-at-home orders, which, in many cases, may have only lasted for a few weeks. Even during that time, people could have still fairly easily shopped at supermarkets, sought medical care, or exercised outdoors. Of course, though, the former two points come with caveats, such that either out of fear of contracting the virus or due to challenges at hospitals or healthcare facilities, many individuals may not have necessarily been able to seek the care they desired (e.g., Anderson et al., 2021). How we shop for groceries has also been significantly altered due to the pandemic with e-commerce, including at-home shopping with same-day grocery delivery services like Instacart and Shipt nearly doubling its total U.S. retail sales in 2020 from 2019 to about 22% (Johnston, 2021).

Where exactly you could go (if you desired to) often varied considerably depending on the policies of where you lived. For instance, if you wanted to eat inside a restaurant in late April 2020 in the State of Georgia, you would have been able to do so (McKibben, 2021). However, that would not have been possible to do in New York—and yet, New York City found a way to reinvent the dining experience with an exponential growth of outdoor dining (Romero, 2021). This highlights how, in many respects, the pandemic was a showcase of resiliency of sorts—at least in the respect of trying to carry out "everyday life" even if it meant having to go through rather unique means to do so. For example, though sports fans were largely unable to physically attend sporting events (particularly in 2020), many times cardboard cutouts of individuals were placed in stands—and, in many cases, a fan could actually pay for a cardboard likeness of themselves to be placed there (Lauterbach, 2020).

These aforesaid points notwithstanding, this is not to suggest that altered plans for events and venues were always possible or even prudent if they had been attempted. Even though the challenges of remote learning in the pandemic were bountiful (and discussed in more detail in the next chapter; Hobbs & Hawkins, 2020), some individuals (like students) may have missed out on events that may have been rites of passage (or social life events that are expected in a sequential way)—like high school proms and graduations for the Class of 2020—that were truly developmentally time-specific and never can be experienced again leaving many such individuals to feel that they were "cheated" out of experiencing them thereby further engendering feelings of loss (WSJ Noted, 2021). Other significant events that actually did take place during the pandemic—like the 2020 Tokyo Summer Olympics (which were initially cancelled but later) held in August 2021—were widely criticized for doing so and may have helped drive a Covid-surge in Japan (Rasheed, 2021).

But, as vaccines became more widely available and dispersed, increasingly, individuals could effectively return to wherever they wanted to go or do whatever they wanted to do—provided that the business or locale in question did not permanently close due to the pandemic (e.g., Simon, 2021). A larger question may be to what degree the pandemic has—or will—cause shifts to both individual behavior (such as health practices; Arora & Grey, 2020) and our collective behavior (such as how and where we travel; van Wee & Witlox, 2021). In many respects, this future dissonance may pit our initial pre-Covid behavioral and attitudinal tendencies against some of our newfound habits that have been developed during or due to the pandemic.

Challenges and Rethinking Urban Life Due to the Pandemic

Continuing a bit with the aforementioned theme of the uncertainty of trying to predict how the pandemic may have reshaped either individual or collective behavior, an important topic to consider has to do with the future of cities and urban life. Florida et al. (2021) contend that though the pandemic is unlikely to radically alter the general scheme of the global city system, the social structure of cities may show some longer-term shifts, particularly as a function of the pandemic's timeline and length. Though this section largely focuses on America's largest city, New York, this analysis also has relevance to larger urban areas in a post-Covid world.

Before we consider some of the developments in New York City post-Covid, let us briefly revisit the era of the 1970s and 1980s where New York City experienced near bankruptcy resulting in profound urban decay and subsequent declines in populations and increases in crime worsened by both the crack and AIDS epidemics (e.g., Dyja, 2021). While New York City gained population in the 2020 Census (though there have been dubious claims about those figures and suggestions that it has since declined; Bhat, 2022), it decidedly did not in the 1980 Census; in fact, between 1970 and 1980, it lost around 800,000 residents. The demographic changes, at that time, reflected a larger retreat from cities to suburban areas and were often fueled by the racially charged dynamic of "white flight" (DeSena & Krase, 2015). Ultimately, a significant tax base that once was, was no more in New York City—and, this trend helped set into motion New York City's near bankruptcy and decline in the 1970s. In the years that followed, New York City would witness its most cataclysmic day—September 11, 2001—resulting in the collapse of the World Trade Center following a terrorist attack where nearly 3,000 individuals were killed. New York City would be tested again a few years later, in 2007, with the start of the Great Recession and a crisis in banking and financial markets (Dyja, 2021).

But, the plight of New York City in a post-Covid world is rather contradictory in many respects. On one hand, New York suffered particularly grievously in the earliest days of the pandemic and has indeed been challenged with its worst economic crisis since the 1970s (Barkan, 2020). On a per-capita basis, in contrast to the peak of the 1918 pandemic surge in New York, the city actually suffered greater losses due to Covid at its peak in the early months of 2020; given this higher death rate with today's vastly improved medical technology, this further highlighted the gravity of the Covid virus (Christensen, 2020). A September 2020 report from then-New York City Mayor Bill de Blasio's office described the deaths emanating from the pandemic in New York City thus far as the "largest mass fatality incident in modern New York City history" (NBC New York, 2020). As America's largest city, it is understandable that a densely populated metropolis would be an ideal location for a contagious virus to spread and thrive. Just as significantly, New York, though, of course, is a major international and national transportation hub. Given that in the early months of the pandemic, international travel was not limited (and Americans could freely travel within the country and abroad), this likely made New York particularly vulnerable to the virus. As was the case virtually across the country, once pandemic lockdowns were established, naturally, most indoor-related entertainment and dining venues were initially shuttered. Though many of the particulars of these limitations varied as the pandemic progressed, these regulations may have been particularly daunting in urban areas dependent on regularly serving large populations. For instance, it wasn't until May 2021 when capacity limitations were no longer placed on restaurants and Broadway shows did not start to reopen until September 2021 (when quite notably, to partake in such activities in New York, proof of vaccination was also instituted; Barron, 2022). Curiously though, the density of urban areas may not have been inherently linked to viral spread and cities—like New York—tend to have far more resources and health facilities to manage the serious challenges posed by Covid (Hamidi et al., 2020).

However, it is clear though that the so-called "City That Never Sleeps" at the very least took a prolonged slumber. Another telling example of how New York took a prolonged pause is how its subways—which typically run at all times—were, in fact, routinely closed overnight for a year in order to provide for regular cleanings (Schoenfeld, 2020). Indeed, national transit ridership fell by about 80% in 2020 from the previous year (Snyder, 2021); notably though, New York City subway ridership was higher in neighborhoods with lower household incomes, higher unemployment, and immigrant populations (NBC New York, 2021).

As an example of further contradictory evidence, on one hand, urban areas (including New York City) continue to flourish and expand its population—while rural areas continue to contract—as further demonstrated by 2020 Census data (Brown, 2021). But, the COVID-19 pandemic felt different and saw an estimated number of 420,000 New Yorkers to leave the city (at least temporarily) between March and May 2020 (Krueger, 2020). In fact, author James Altucher (2020) published an essay in August 2020 that received a significant amount of media and Internet attention with its provocative title and declaration "NYC IS DEAD FOREVER. HERE'S WHY." In this essay, among other key reasons, he cites the perceived decline in individuals wishing to live or visit in New York City in the wake of the pandemic (Smith, 2020). Others also seriously questioned the value of cities given the newfound reality that many who held professional jobs could work from home—or anywhere—and avoid the high prices often associated with urban life (e.g., Lahart, 2020). If larger corporations or wealthier individuals decided to leave New York in great numbers, the concern is that a similar sort of paradigm like what occurred in New York in the 1970s financial crisis (e.g., Dyja, 2021) could take hold. Indeed, there have been voiced concerns that the pandemic may have started a similar downturn in quality of life for the city both during its initial months (Barron,

2020) and nearly two years following the devastating initial Covid surge in New York City (Wilson et al., 2022) that parallel the aforementioned time period.

At this time, it is impossible to discern exactly how the pandemic will change urban life—or New York City, in particular. Indeed, there remain many contradictory patterns for New York City. On one hand, after suffering a bit of a downturn immediately at the start of the pandemic, New York City's housing market (especially for high end-housing) remains quite robust (though there has been consideration of trying to use real estate, like former hotels, as affordable housing; Gonen, 2020). Yet, there has been cause for concern in its commercial real estate market (Krauth, 2021). The pandemic may have exacerbated trends over whether it is truly necessary to commute into the core (e.g., downtown or midtown) of a city in order to do one's work (Brean, 2020). Naturally, if there are fewer individuals and companies working in a city, this decreases the need for such office space (such as in New York City where it hadn't had as much vacant office space in 30 years in early 2021; Kosik, 2021)— and with it, commercial spaces (such as shops and restaurants) may lose their ability to operate without such a consistent base of customers (Hutchison, 2021). Similar questions abound as to when and how tourists and visitors' habits to cities may have been altered due to the pandemic: Just because one can, for instance, attend a Broadway show again, does not necessarily mean one will do so (e.g., Noonan, 2021).

As noted previously, population trends do not suggest that Americans are retreating *en masse* from cities—in fact, the opposite is largely true. In the 2020 Census, the New York City metropolitan area showed some surprising population growth, even though there is also some evidence that thousands of New Yorkers (and other residents from large American urban areas) fled during the pandemic (Tate, 2020). But what do these conflicting trends mean for New York (and cities, more generally)? As difficult as it is to forecast such changes, the pandemic—at the least—reminded us of the inherent vulnerabilities and fragilities of cities. By their very definition, cities offer and require shared space—in offices, dwellings, entertainment venues, and transportation hubs. The presence of a highly transmissible novel virus challenged the safety of such places. The degree to which (and how) individuals continue to navigate such spaces will be (to some degree) a function of the state of the virus itself; that is, if transmission rates remain low and vaccines continue to be effective, it is likely that individuals will increasingly be comfortable in such environments. But, urban design and architecture must clearly be even more mindful of these biologic threats post-pandemic. How cities recover from the pandemic may ultimately be decided by who exactly chooses to remain in them (Pearlstein, 2020). Perhaps though the larger question to entertain is what purpose should our cities have post-pandemic particularly if individuals have greater flexibility in regard to how they work and where they live (Lahart, 2020).

Challenges Present in Rural Life

In contrast to urban centers, at some level, rural locations would have seemed to have been an almost natural choice to try to somehow "flee" the effects of the virus and pandemic (as many city-dwellers did indeed opt to do). In hindsight, such thinking may have been faulty insomuch that the very nature of a pandemic inherently suggests an easily widespread disease amongst a population irrespective of location (Caron, 2020). In many respects, such decisions may have been guided by cognitive heuristics that may have made some feel that a sparsely populated area would somehow offer greater protection from the virus than an urban metropolis teeming with people (Liò et al., 2013). But again, a person could have been holed up in the hinterlands of New England, as an example, and still have gotten infected by coming across a sole person.

The pandemic served as a reminder that many rural locations often face systemic challenges to providing healthcare in contrast to urban areas (such as potentially more limited means of specialized care; Ricketts, 2000). But, not all was necessarily dour (or had to be) with respect to the prospect of care during the pandemic. The State of West Virginia offers a telling example of this point. When Covid vaccines started to be disseminated in early 2021, West Virginia was hailed as a model for efficient and effective vaccine distribution particularly in contrast to the chaotic nature of how vaccines were distributed across urban America (Ducharme, 2021). In the first few months of 2021, trying to secure an appointment for a vaccination proved to be a daunting task for many. In most cases, appointments had to be made online and the ways and means of doing so were often confusing or unclear (e.g., Otterman, 2021). For instance, in trying to secure an online vaccine appointment for my elderly mother, it was essential to routinely refresh one's Internet browser and hope that by the time all of the relevant personal information was entered, the appointment slot was still available. The larger point is that those who were particularly in critical need of a vaccine—such as the elderly or the infirmed—may not necessarily have had the technological or physical ability to have easily secured such appointments. The State of West Virginia was able to bypass these hurdles by employing a clever policy of distributing vaccines to largely local community drugstores; the drugstore staff, in turn, was able to personally connect with those most in need of the vaccine and ensured access to these vulnerable populations (Massey, 2021).

Though 2021 started on a positive note regarding vaccinations for West Virginia, it did not end as such, given that this State has routinely ranked as one of the least vaccinated in all of America—despite many generous incentives that the State has offered to its citizens (such as prizes and related promotions). The reason for this unfortunate turn of events is likely related to many of the political dimensions previously discussed in this book. Indeed, rural and Republican-leaning voters were often least eager to get vaccinated (if at all) once it was available (Owens, 2021). West Virginia is one of America's more rural and lightly populated States. It also proved to be the State that gave Donald Trump his biggest margin of victory in 2020 over Joe Biden save for the least populated State of Wyoming. In other words, the reality of life in rural, conservative States—like West Virginia—during the pandemic was that these areas were more likely to contain individuals who were least likely to adhere to preventative strategies (such as mask-wearing and social distancing) and were less likely to get vaccinated (Enten, 2021). Indeed, it was in these areas of the country that largely helped to fuel the summer and fall 2021 surge of the Delta variant (Cuadros et al., 2022). It is important to clarify, though, that it would be inappropriate to conclude that living in a rural area, in and of itself, was the chief reason why one would necessarily hold conservative views or potentially act in accordance with the pandemic-related health decisions described above (e.g., Van Nostrand et al., 2022).

To reflect on this chapter, the pandemic certainly provides all of us with a chance to reconsider how we engaged with our physical environments during this time—and how perhaps these engagements impacted us individually. This chapter is another reminder too of how and where we live can have great consequences for our general adjustment and quality of life we experience. More broadly though, the pandemic offers a chance for urban planners, governmental agencies, health practitioners, and environmental psychologists a greater opportunity to examine psychological adjustment in various environmental contexts, particularly cities (McCunn, 2021). Perhaps too, the pandemic has highlighted both how nature itself can be a potential source of healing (e.g., Chaudhury and Banerjee, 2020) but also in need of great protection (e.g., Poursadeqiyan et al., 2020).

References

Altucher, J. (2020, August 13). NYC is dead forever. Here's why. *LinkedIn.* https://www.linkedin.com/pulse/nyc-dead-forever-heres-why-james-altucher

Anderson, K. E., McGinty, E. E., Presskreischer, R., & Barry, C. L. (2021). Reports of forgone medical care among US adults during the initial phase of the COVID-19 pandemic. *JAMA Network Open, 4*(1), e2034882-e2034882. https://doi.org/10.1001/jamanetworkopen.2020.34882

Arora, T., & Grey, I. (2020). Health behaviour changes during COVID-19 and the potential consequences: A mini-review. *Journal of Health Psychology, 25*(9), 1155-1163. https://doi.org/10.1177/1359105320937053

Barkan, R. (2020, August 26). How can NYC escape its worst economic crisis in decades? *Gothamist*. https://gothamist.com/news/how-can-nyc-escape-its-worst-economic-crisis-decades

Barron, J. (2022, March 17). Two years of the pandemic: New York looks back. *The New York Times*. https://www.nytimes.com/2022/03/17/nyregion/two-years-of-the-pandemic-new-york-looks-back.html

Barron, S. (2020, Autumn). Anarchy in New York? *City Journal*. https://www.city-journal.org/anarchy-in-new-york

Bhat, S. (2022, May 31). NYC's population plummeted during peak COVID — And it's still likely shrinking. *The City*. https://www.thecity.nyc/2022/5/31/23145072/nycs-population-plummeted-during-peak-covid-and-its-still-likely-shrinking

Brean, J. (2020, May 30). In the new downtown future, devoid of office workers, every day could be Sunday. *National Post*. https://nationalpost.com/news/in-the-new-downtown-future-devoid-of-office-workers-every-day-could-be-Sunday

Brown, M. (2021, August 12). Takeaways from the US census: A slower growing but more multiracial society, as cities outpace rural areas. *USA Today*. https://www.usatoday.com/story/news/politics/2021/08/12/takeaways-2020-census-rural-urban-population-divides/5493030001/

Caron, C. (2021, December 7). Are cities a safe place to live during a pandemic? *The New York Times*. https://www.nytimes.com/2020/12/07/well/live/coronavirus-cities-safe.html

Chaudhury, P., & Banerjee, D. (2020). "Recovering with nature": A review of ecotherapy and implications for the COVID-19 pandemic. *Frontiers in Public Health, 8*, 604440. https://doi.org/10.3389/fpubh.2020.604440

Christensen, J. (2020, August 14). Deaths during the coronavirus surge in New York City recall the peak of the 1918 flu pandemic. *CNN*. https://www.cnn.com/2020/08/14/health/covid19-1918-flu-deaths-new-york-wellness/index.html

Cuadros, D. F., Miller, F. D., Awad, S., Coule, P., & MacKinnon, N. J. (2022). Analysis of vaccination rates and new COVID-19 infections by US county, July-August 2021. *JAMA Network Open, 5*(2), e2147915-e2147915. doi:10.1001/jamanetworkopen.2021.47915

DeSena, J., & Krase, J. (2015). Brooklyn revisited: An illustrated view from the street 1970 to the present. *Urbanities—Journal of Urban Ethnography, 5*(2), 3-19.

Ducharme, J. (2021, June 29). What the U.S. can learn about health care from this West Virginia county's successful vaccine rollout. *Time*. https://time.com/6075430/west-virginia-covid-19-vaccine-rollout/

Dyja, T. (2021). *New York, New York: Four decades of success, excess, and transformation*. Simon & Schuster.

Enten, H. (2021, September 26). How West Virginia became a Covid-19 disaster. *CNN*. https://www.cnn.com/2021/09/26/politics/west-virginia-covid-analysis/index.html

Florida, R., Rodríguez-Pose, A., & Storper, M. (2021). Cities in a post-COVID world. *Urban Studies*. https://doi.org/10.1177/00420980211018072

Gonen, Y. (2020, June 25). Pandemic-emptied hotels could become affordable housing, city officials suggest. *The City.* https://www.thecity.nyc/housing/2020/6/25/21303923/hotels-could-become-affordable-housing-in-nyc

Hamidi, S., Sabouri, S., & Ewing, R. (2020). Does density aggravate the COVID-19 pandemic? Early findings and lessons for planners. *Journal of the American Planning Association, 86*(4), 495-509. https://doi.org/10.1080/01944363.2020.1777891

Hobbs, T. D., & Hawkins, L. (2020, June 5). The results are in for remote learning: It didn't work. *The Wall Street Journal.* https://www.wsj.com/articles/schools-coronavirus-remote-learning-lockdown-tech-11591375078

Hutchison, P. (2021, January 26). The end of offices? New York's business districts face uncertain future. *Yahoo! News.* https://news.yahoo.com/end-offices-yorks-business-districts-022038475.html

Johnston, P. (2021, April 7). Retailers, delivery services adapt to altered landscape. *National Retail Federation.* https://nrf.com/blog/retailers-delivery-services-adapt-altered-landscape

Kosik, A. (2021, April 22). New York City hasn't had this much empty office space in three decades. *CNN.* https://www.cnn.com/2021/04/22/business/office-space-new-york-city-downturn/index.html

Krauth, D. (2021, March 15). The old New York is gone: Here's what NYC will look like next. *ABC 7 New York.* https://abc7ny.com/health/the-old-new-york-is-gone-heres-what-happens-next/10408252/

Krueger, A. (2020, June 5). The agonizing question: Is New York City worth it anymore? *The New York Times.* https://www.nytimes.com/2020/06/05/nyregion/coronavirus-leaving-nyc.html

Lahart, J. (2020, June 6). Who needs cities when we all work from home? *The Wall Street Journal.* https://www.wsj.com/articles/who-needs-cities-when-we-all-work-from-home-11591394516

Lauterbach, J. (2020, August 3). What MLB teams are charging for cardboard cutouts. *Newsday.* https://www.newsday.com/sports/baseball/mets/mlb-cardboard-cutout-fan-program-prices-1.46903145

Liò, P., Lucia, B., Nguyen, V. A., & Kitchovitch, S. (2013). Risk perception, heuristics and epidemic spread. In P. Manfredi & A. D'Onofrio (Eds.), *Modeling the interplay between human behavior and the spread of infectious diseases* (pp. 139-152). Springer.

Massey, D. (2021, March 4). A West Virginia pharmacist on how the state became a vaccine success story. *Vox.* https://www.vox.com/first-person/2021/3/4/22313540/covid-19-vaccine-west-virginia

McCunn, L. J. (2021). The importance of nature to city living during the COVID-19 pandemic: Considerations and goals from environmental psychology. *Cities & Health, 5*(sup1), S223-S226. https://doi.org/10.1080/23748834.2020.1795385

McKibben, B. (2021, May 3). With the last remaining restrictions lifted, Georgia is officially open for business. *Eater.* https://atlanta.eater.com/2021/4/8/22373375/georgia-governor-lifts-capacity-restrictions-restaurants-bars-lifts-ban-large-gatherings-covid19

Melore, C. (2021, April 16). Doing laundry 'highlight of week' for third of Americans beyond bored from pandemic isolation. *Study Finds.* https://www. studyfinds.org/doing-laundry-highlight-of-week-pandemic-isolation/

NBC New York (2020, September 18). COVID-19 is 'largest mass fatality incident' in modern NYC history, new report says. *NBC New York.* https://www.nbcnewyork. com/news/local/covid-19-is-largest-mass-fatality-incident-in-modern-nyc-history-new-report-says/2624598/

NBC New York (2021, March 19). Outlying neighborhoods make up largest return in NYC subway ridership. *NBC New York.* https://www.nbcnewyork.com/news/local/outlying-neighborhoods-make-up-largest-return-in-nyc-subway-ridership/2953680/

Noonan, P. (2021, February 25). The old New York won't come back. *The Wall Street Journal.* https://www.wsj.com/articles/the-old-new-york-wont-come-back-11614296201

Otterman, S. (2021, February 9). N.Y.'s vaccine websites weren't working, so he built a new one for $50. *The New York Times.* https://www.nytimes.com/2021/02/09/world/nys-vaccine-websites-werent-working-so-he-built-a-new-one-for-50.html

Owens, C. (2021, April 9). America may be close to hitting a vaccine wall. *Axios.* https://www.axios.com/america-coronavirus-vaccines-republicans-rural-states-34755cbf-384e-4539-bb45-68a775581f6f.html

Pearlstein, S. (2020, September 22). Not so fast, urban exodus: Coronavirus could make New York and San Francisco great places to live again. *The Washington Post.* https://www.washingtonpost.com/business/2020/09/22/commercial-real-estate-covid-new-york/

Poursadeqiyan, M., Bazrafshan, E., & Arefi, M. F. (2020). Review of environmental challenges and pandemic crisis of Covid-19. *Journal of Education and Health Promotion, 9,* 250. https://doi.org/10.4103/jehp.jehp_420_20

Rasheed, Z. (2021, August 10). Did the Tokyo Olympics drive Japan's COVID-19 surge? *Al Jazeera.* https://www.aljazeera.com/news/2021/8/10/did-the-tokyo-olympics-fuel-japans-covid-19-surge

Ricketts, T. C. (2000). The changing nature of rural health care. *Annual Review of Public Health, 21*(1), 639-657. https://doi.org/10.1146/annurev.publhealth.21.1.639

Romero, D. (2021, October 10). NYC outdoor dining a 'huge game-changer' for COVID-hit restaurants as opposition grows. *Yahoo! News.* https://news.yahoo.com/nyc-outdoor-dining-a-huge-game-changer-for-restaurants-but-oppositions-grows-153151326.html

Schoenfeld, A. (2020, July 30). How safe is the New York City subway right now? *Newsweek.* https://www.newsweek.com/how-safe-new-york-city-subway-right-now-1521844

Simon, R. (2021, April 16). Covid-19's toll on U.S. business? 200,000 extra closures in pandemic's first year. *The Wall Street Journal.* https://www.wsj.com/articles/covid-19s-toll-on-u-s-business-200-000-extra-closures-in-pandemics-first-year-11618580619

Smith, J. (2020, August 17). New York is finished! Big Apple born-and-bred entrepreneur pens devastating blog on why city will never recover after being devastated by Covid, looting and a crime wave. *Daily Mail.* https://www.

dailymail.co.uk/news/article-8635857/Why-NYC-WONT-survive-coronavirus-Entrepreneur-outlines-city-forever-changed.html#comments

Snyder, T. (2021, May 27). Policy hackathon: Can public transit recover from Covid-19? *Politico.* https://www.politico.com/news/2021/05/27/covid-public-transit-hackathon-489983

Tate, K. (2020, December 13). Is this the end of cities in America? *The Hill.* https://thehill.com/opinion/finance/530040-is-this-the-end-of-cities-in-america

Van Nostrand, E., Robinson, T. J., & Palumbo, A. J. (2022). Why aren't Mountain State folks getting the shot? Health literacy, COVID-19, and vaccination rates in West Virginia counties. *West Virginia Law Review, 124*(3), 709-740.

van Wee, B., & Witlox, F. (2021). COVID-19 and its long-term effects on activity participation and travel behaviour: A multiperspective view. *Journal of Transport Geography, 95,* 103144. https://doi.org/10.1016/j.jtrangeo.2021.103144

Wilson, W., Marcius, C. R., & Schweber, N. (2022, January 23). A grim January leaves some New Yorkers fearful for the city's future. *The New York Times.* https://www.nytimes.com/2022/01/23/nyregion/nypd-shooting.html

WSJ Noted. (2021, April 27). The Class of 2020 is still feeling the impact of lost graduation. *WSJ Noted.* https://www.wsj.com/articles/the-class-of-2020-is-still-feeling-the-impact-of-lost-graduation-11619549447

CHAPTER NINE
Online and Virtual (Learning) Worlds

This chapter examines how online communications, particularly school and work-based modalities, increased greatly during the pandemic. The possible individual and societal consequences of this paradigm are also considered.

The Critical (Yet Contradictory) Role of the Internet

Of course, historically, pandemics occurred well before the Internet. It is quite compelling to look at photographs from the era of the 1918 flu pandemic, including the masks worn by individuals (both inside and outside) and the public health publications designed to promote good hygiene (e.g., Wilson, 2020). While these sorts of images and realities provide a sort of visual link to that pandemic, a clearly distinguishing characteristic in our current-day pandemic has been that most individuals have had regular Internet access. Particularly in the earliest phases of the pandemic where lockdowns and "stay at home" governmental orders were commonplace, it is difficult to imagine how most individuals could not carry out routine functions without the Internet—as, of course, was not the case regarding the 1918 pandemic (Lovelace, 2020a). Frankly, most of the online activities individuals may have been doing during the pandemic—such as working, learning, communicating with others, shopping, and seeking games or entertainment—were routinely done prior to the pandemic. But, it is the degree to which these activities have been done online since the pandemic that has markedly increased. As an example, in 2019, 81% of consumers never purchased groceries online, whereas 79% did so at some point during the first year of the pandemic (Morgan, 2020).

And yet, online communication has repeatedly been shown to be fraught with a mix of potentially beneficial and deleterious consequences for individuals and their relationships (such as miscommunication; e.g., Miller, 2018)—and the pandemic has proven to be no different. For instance, though individuals had countless technological means to stay technologically connected, the concern or inability to meet in person posed a challenge for many friendships; perhaps more insidiously, by continuously staying in touch with others on social media, many may have discovered views from close others (e.g., shunning mask wearing) that were diametrically opposed to their worldview thereby potentially posing a serious threat to the relationship (Hamedy & Ebrahimji, 2020). This is not to suggest that increased online communication during Covid led to relationship breakdown in an absolute sense—but it may have at least altered our personal expectations for our relationships (Wasson Simpson & Muise, 2022). In fact, there is evidence that online contact with friends was beneficial during the pandemic in terms of lower levels of loneliness, anxiety, and depression provided that adults were generally satisfied with the nature of their exchanges (Juvonen et al., 2021). Despite the means and availability to communicate with others virtually, many adolescents and young adults still felt a sense of social isolation (McKinlay et al., 2022); this paradox seems to define the fundamental relationship that many adolescents have with social media in the wake of the pandemic (Hamilton et al., 2022).

Even if one did not necessarily encounter overt problems while conducting online communications, business, or other transactions, many individuals have reported a sense of virtual meeting fatigue where they felt as if they needed to be continuously connected to their Internet-based devices (Epstein, 2020). A cross-sectional study of Italian academics found that greater use of technology and a history of poorer physical and psychological health tended to be associated with greater reports of such fatigue; women and those with minor-age children were particularly likely to indicate greater online fatigue as well (Bonanomi et al., 2021).

One of the most profound ways that the Internet has been used during the pandemic was to say goodbye to dying loved ones and to attend virtual funerals. Here again, the Internet may have offered some solace to those who otherwise would not have been able to attend due to Covid, but others may have struggled with this technology (Muturi et al., 2020) or may not have necessarily felt that such communication provided the appropriate means to express their bereavement (Burrell & Selman, 2020). More broadly, Walsh (2020) wonders with some consternation about how this dramatic turn to technology may bring larger implications for a potentially greater withdrawal from public life, including how we conduct schooling and work.

Rethinking the Office and the Digital Divide (of Work)

Though many office workers (including about half of all adult respondents who were vaccinated in a March 2021 American Psychological Association survey) reported being wary about returning to their office for work and fears about the virus may persist, the increased flexibility associated with not having to commute to and remain at a particular place at a particular time has caused many to question and rethink what work should "look like" as we progress past the early months and years of the pandemic (Chuck, 2021). While there may be a myriad of tensions between those who are effectively forced to return to the office, even those who continue to work online or with a hybrid model (of blended online and face-to-face work) may still face inequities (such as perceived favoritism for reporting to the office or childcare difficulties; e.g., Giorgi et al.,

2020; Galanti et al., 2021). There are also very significant economic considerations for both employees and employers with respect to what precisely defines the post-pandemic "office." Employees often face challenging issues about their pay and tax rate depending on where they live (or have moved to) and the physical space (if any) that defines their office; employers not only have had to ensure their workers have their necessary materials (e.g., computer equipment) but have also been faced with the dilemma of possibly downsizing their physical office space (Vasel, 2021). Even though not every worker will be able (or want to) necessarily work remotely indefinitely post-Covid, there is a growing consensus that greater workplace flexibility and diversity in modalities of work (e.g., shared workplaces, commuter hub offices) may become more of a norm, particularly in many traditional white-collar professional jobs (Hirschfeld, 2020).

The Dynamics of Remote/Online Schooling

Much of the tension behind remote and online schooling has pitted two basic fundamental realities that largely held much credence. On one hand, particularly when the vaccine was not widely available to both adults and children, there was much evidence to support that bringing groups of people together in a room—such as in a traditional classroom—without any preventative means of viral transmission was, naturally, a clear risk for all involved. Prior to the vaccine's availability, a middle school teacher named "Sarah" gained national attention for a prominent Facebook post that summarized her concerns at the time. Some of her most powerful concerns were put this way:

> …I am so sick of being expected to be some sort of martyr because I decided to be a teacher…I love teaching. I love my students. But guess what? I don't love my students or teaching more than I love my own kids or the rest of my family or my own life. I will not sacrifice myself and I won't feel guilty… (ABC 7 New York, 2020, p. 4).

One way to effectively eliminate that particular risk was to completely hold classes in an online or remote setting. The concern about the virus notwithstanding, online education had been increasingly in effect over the past few decades prior to the pandemic but never to the extent that occurred as a result of the pandemic. The pandemic revealed that entirely online schooling may not be beneficial to all students. For instance, in a comprehensive survey conducted by NBC News and the non-profit group Challenge Success, high school students who were completely online in the fall of 2020 were much more likely to report greater stress, stress-related ailments, less support, and greater amounts of work than peers who were in the traditional physical classroom (and these results were particularly pronounced amongst females and students of color; Einhorn, 2021). Other additional studies suggest that it is truly difficult to tease apart the influence of the online learning modality from the more general adverse effects of the pandemic. The sudden shift to remote or online learning may have indeed been a negative experience for students, particularly if they had previously been unaccustomed to such learning modalities. For instance, in a study of Saudi Arabian college students, Azmi et al. (2022) found that students who viewed such learning as boring or worrisome tended to show increased depression. Another investigation with American college students found that many technical aspects that were often part of remote or online classes, such as replying to chat questions or unmuting audio, were often associated with anxiety (Pennino et al., 2022). But again, to offer some caution interpreting those findings, many personal characteristics (such as higher neuroticism, external locus of control, gender and race) may have also been significant reasons why the move to online learning was stressful to some (Clabaugh et al., 2021).

To further highlight the point that it may not necessarily at all be the case that online education per se has served as a potential source of stress for many students, the pandemic has raised much concern that children and adolescents have had to turn to the Internet both for their schoolwork and as a source of downtime recreation at the expense of face-to-face schooling, social interactions with peers, and pursuing other personally meaningful activities (such as sports). To further darken this paradigm, many such minors have also had to do so while contending with larger familial stress; in turn, this heightened stress might have enhanced health concerns like obesity risks (MacGillis, 2021). Psychologist Maggie Mulqueen (2020) cautioned that the broader debate about how to conduct schooling in the pandemic missed the larger point that students have been functioning in a world that is decidedly "unnatural;" even if mask-wearing and social distancing has been critical to curtail viral spread (and largely remained in schools for as long as there was significant viral spread; Lovelace, 2020b), it can be a developmentally disorienting experience to students who have been likely also coping with familial struggles and the larger societal losses associated with the pandemic.

The balance between keeping teachers, staff, and students safe from the virus versus weighing educational, personal, and emotional needs of students—particularly in K-12 environments—has been an issue virtually from the earliest months of the pandemic. Images from a Georgia high school in August 2020 of students shoulder-to-shoulder in hallways en route to class without masks received national attention underscoring the clear health risks associated with trying to run schools under pre-Covid conditions when it was revealed that at least nine individuals were infected from this school (Stelloh & Alexander, 2020). The very nature of a pandemic means that the decision to gather individuals themselves makes not just those individuals at risk but also poses serious considerations and concerns for their respective family members (e.g., parents and spouses) and their larger communities. In August 2020, writer Kathi Valeii (2020) discussed her decision to keep her children at home given that there was no available vaccine at the time. The latter point is particularly notable given—even at that point in time—there already was much clamour and pushback by both some parents and larger communal and political figures to effectively conduct schooling as it was done pre-Covid. Regrettably, political ideologies skewed how Americans viewed the question of how—or whether to open schools. In a July 2020 AP-NORC poll, 44% of Democrats but only 14% of Republicans felt that schools should not open at all; at the other extreme, 17% of Republicans felt that schools should be open as usual, but only 1% of Democrats replied the same. On a hopeful note of agreement, the majority of all adults (50% of Democrats and 43% of Republicans) believed that schools should be open with "major adjustment" (Binkley & Fingerhut, 2020). But, a significant part of the problem, particularly preceding the start of the 2020-2021 school year, was a generic pronouncement from the Trump administration that children should just go back to school often without any clearly articulated way of explaining how this could or should be accomplished safely (e.g., Calarco, 2020); further, there were reports that top Trump White House officials tried to pressure the CDC to minimize the potential health risks of returning back to school (Richards, 2020).

American colleges had other considerations to contend with such as lawsuits designed to recoup tuition for holding fully online classes when they largely went remote at the start of the pandemic (e.g., Bennett, 2020) or a personal belief such online course offerings were somehow inferior (e.g., Owens, 2020). The actual merits of these lawsuits notwithstanding, Belkin (2020) picks up on the larger theme of student perceptions about the costs of college and time spent earning a given degree post-Covid. While he does not contend that the traditional college experience will ever disappear, he does suggest that the pandemic has particularly highlighted the need to recognize that this experience is not necessarily beneficial to all and that more specialized, vocational-focused training may be a more suitable option to many students in this post-Covid environment. In June 2020, Susan Dynarski, a professor of education, public policy and economics made the point that the potential health risks to college members and the larger community were not worth bringing students en masse back to campus. But then she posed the following question with a clear response:

> Given the enormous health risks involved in bringing students back, why are so many colleges promising to open their campuses? The answer is simple: Their financial survival depends on it. Many four-year colleges,

especially the most selective schools, provide not just classroom learning but also the social experience of clubs, athletics, culture, politics and professional networking (Dynarski, 2020, p. 2).

Her analysis should force us to question—or perhaps realize—what education is or should be. While the technology is largely available to deliver educational materials and to even socialize online, the pandemic also highlighted the in person social nature of education—including all of its financially related incentives for schools and colleges. Sociologist Tressie McMillan Cottom furthered this view by adding that the pandemic has exacerbated the customer model of higher education by showcasing the value of the so-called "college experience" which is more rooted in on-campus rather than virtual experiences (Doherty et al., 2021).

Like K-12 schools, colleges though had to weigh the challenges of how to conduct their classes. In many respects, colleges were largely placed in a Catch-22 situation insomuch that many of them had dubious reopening plans—particularly during the first full semester following the initial lockdowns to offer classes in fall 2020—that may have been (implicitly or not) influenced by political and financial considerations (Mitchell, 2020); indeed, even before the pandemic, many colleges were facing undergraduate enrollment declines due to demographics that the pandemic may have exacerbated (Lorin, 2020). Many of these plans also purportedly tried to remind students of the importance of their personal behavior—or even blame them for it—often without clear ways or means of monitoring such behaviors or somehow penalizing faulty actions (Marcus & Gold, 2020). Regehr and Goel (2020) offered some important reflections on the vast challenges that colleges have had to face during the pandemic; they contend that though colleges plan for crisis management situations, most colleges had to face an unprecedented situation of shutting down their campuses and moving all of their classes online—which for some students and faculty may have been a more unique challenge. In the months that followed there was prolonged uncertainty followed by a restart of sorts where campuses were largely opened and many face-to-face classes resumed, particularly following the introduction and availability of the vaccine—though there were also serious questions as to how well or honest universities had been in their reporting of cases (Seltzer, 2020) as well as often unclear testing plans (McAuliff et al., 2020). But, unfortunately (as again shown by the January 2022 Omicron surge; Anderson, 2022), returning back to traditional campus life is not necessarily as simple to do as a function of the degree that the virus remains circulating in communities as well as the presence of vaccine hesitancy amongst students or staff.

To reiterate an important point from this chapter, let us be clear that Internet-based modalities of communication had already been entrenched in society well before the pandemic—though it truly advanced the degree and way by which we make use of such technologies. When humans learn a new way of behaving, it is very difficult to unlearn such forms of behavior. To be clear, the early weeks and months of the Covid pandemic are qualitatively different than the realities of life two years later. As many societal sectors have tried to reincorporate ways of functioning that existed prior to the pandemic (such as physically returning to school or work), to the degree that some of the technological shifts made during the pandemic adversely impacted individuals (e.g., K-12 students and parents wanting in person instruction and socialization), these pre-pandemic returns to behavior were necessary. However, the pandemic should at least cause us to reevaluate our relationship with technology in terms of when it may or may not be an appropriate substitute for in person communication or connection.

References

ABC 7 New York. (2020, July 21). 'I will not sacrifice myself,' says teacher fed up with back-to-school debate. *ABC 7 New York.* https://abc7ny.com/teacher-fed-up-back-to-school-plan-b/6327038/

Anderson, N. (2022, January 8). Omicron forces short winter courses to go online at many colleges. *The Washington Post.* https://www.washingtonpost.com/education/2022/01/08/omicron-online-college-winter-courses/

Azmi, F. M., Khan, H. N., & Azmi, A. M. (2022). The impact of virtual learning on students' educational behavior and pervasiveness of depression among university students due to the COVID-19 pandemic. *Globalization and Health, 18,* 1-9. https://doi.org/10.1186/s12992-022-00863-z

Belkin, D. (2020, November 12). Is this the end of college as we know it? *The Wall Street Journal.* https://www.wsj.com/articles/is-this-the-end-of-college-as-we-know-it-11605196909

Bennett, P. (2020, August 2). Student files class action lawsuit against Kent State to recoup tuition and fees. *KentWired.* http://www.kentwired.com/latest_updates/article_319a3204-d528-11ea-a90a-efd37cd61d8d.html

Binkley, C., & Fingerhut, H. (2020, July 21). AP-NORC poll: Very few Americans back full school reopening. *AP News.* https://apnews.com/article/virus-outbreak-politics-lifestyle-ma-state-wire-only-on-ap-b133f482b2eba88f8bd733e2d15d13ae

Bonanomi, A., Facchin, F., Barello, S., & Villani, D. (2021). Prevalence and health correlates of onine fatigue: A cross-sectional study on the Italian academic community during the COVID-19 pandemic. *PLOS ONE, 16*(10), e0255181. https://doi.org/10.1371/journal.pone.0255181

Burrell, A., & Selman, L. E. (2020). How do funeral practices impact bereaved relatives' mental health, grief and bereavement? A mixed methods review with implications for COVID-19. *OMEGA-Journal of Death and Dying,* 0030222820941296. https://doi.org/10.1177/0030222820941296

Calarco, J. (2020, July 15). What is Betsy DeVos thinking? *The New York Times.* https://www.nytimes.com/2020/07/15/opinion/coronavirus-school-reopen -devos.html

Chuck, E. (2021, April 5). Office buildings are opening back up. Not all employees want to return. *NBC News.* https://www.nbcnews.com/news/us-news/office-buildings-are-opening-back-not-all-employees-want-return-n 1262647

Clabaugh, A., Duque, J. F., & Fields, L. J. (2021). Academic stress and emotional well-being in United States college students following onset of the COVID-19 pandemic. *Frontiers in Psychology, 12,* 628787. https://doi.org/10.3389/fpsyg. 2021.628787

Doherty, M., Gilman, N., Harris, A., McMillan Cottom, T., Newfield, C., & Shenk, T. (2021, Fall). Academia after the pandemic: A roundtable on how COVID-19 has changed American universities. *Dissent.* https://www.dissentmagazine. org/article/academia-after-the-pandemic

Dynarski, S. (2020, June 29). College is worth it, but campus isn't. *The New York Times.* https://www.nytimes.com/2020/06/29/business/college-campus-coronavirus-danger.html

Einhorn, E. (2021, February 15). Remote students are more stressed than their peers in the classroom, study shows. *NBC News.* https://www.nbcnews.com/ news/education/remote-students-are-more-stressed-their-peers-classroom -study-shows-n1257632

Epstein, H. A. B. (2020). Virtual meeting fatigue. *Journal of Hospital Librarianship, 20*(4), 356-360. https://doi.org/10.1080/15323269.2020.1819758

Galanti, T., Guidetti, G., Mazzei, E., Zappalà, S., & Toscano, F. (2021). Work from home during the COVID-19 outbreak: The impact on employees' remote work productivity, engagement, and stress. *Journal of Occupational and Environmental Medicine, 63*(7), e426-e432. https://doi.org/10.1097/JOM.0000000000002236

Giorgi, G., Lecca, L. I., Alessio, F., Finstad, G. L., Bondanini, G., Lulli, L. G., Arcangeli, G., & Mucci, N. (2020). COVID-19-related mental health effects in the workplace: A narrative review. *International Journal of Environmental Research and Public Health, 17*(21), 7857. https://doi.org/10.3390/ijerph17217857

Hamedy, S., & Ebrahimji, A. (2020, December 15). The pandemic has destroyed friendships and divided families. *CNN.* https://www.cnn.com/2020/12/15/us/ pandemic-rift-friendships-wellness-trnd/index.html

Hamilton, J. L., Nesi, J., & Choukas-Bradley, S. (2022). Reexamining social media and socioemotional well-being among adolescents through the lens of the COVID-19 pandemic: A theoretical review and directions for future research. *Perspectives on Psychological Science, 17*(3), 662-679. https://doi.org/ 10.1177/17456916211014189

Hirschfeld, A. (2020, June 4). What will your office look like after coronavirus? *InsideHook.* https://www.insidehook.com/article/news-opinion/what-will-your-office-look-like-after-coronavirus

Juvonen, J., Schacter, H. L., & Lessard, L. M. (2021). Connecting electronically with friends to cope with isolation during COVID-19 pandemic. *Journal of Social and Personal Relationships, 38*(6), 1782-1799. https://doi.org/10.1177/02654 075219984

Lorin, J. (2020, October 15). New students at U.S. colleges drop, worsening campus crisis. *Bloomberg.* https://www.bloombergquint.com/onweb/new-students-at-u-s-colleges-decline-worsening-campus-crisis

Lovelace, B., Jr. (2020a, September 28). Medical historian compares the coronavirus to the 1918 flu pandemic: Both were highly political. *CNBC.* https://www.cnbc.com/2020/09/28/comparing-1918-flu-vs-coronavirus.html

Lovelace, B., Jr., (2020b, August 19). Scientists warn it may be years before students can return to school without masks, social distancing. *CNBC.* https://www.cnbc.com/2020/08/19/coronavirus-scientists-warn-it-may-take-years-before-students-return-to-normal-schooling.html

MacGillis, A. (2021, March 8). The lost year: What the pandemic cost teenagers. *ProPublica.* https://www.propublica.org/article/the-lost-year-what-the-pandemic-cost-teenagers

Marcus, J., & Gold, J. (2020, July 21). Colleges are getting ready to blame their students. *The Atlantic.* https://www.theatlantic.com/ideas/archive/2020/07/colleges-are-getting-ready-blame-their-students/614410/

McAuliff, M., Valdivia, S. M., KBIA, Herman, C., Side Effects Public Media, & O'Neill, S. (2020, August 21). Swab, spit, stay home? College coronavirus testing plans are all over the map. *Kaiser Health News.* https://khn.org/news/swab-spit-stay-home-college-coronavirus-testing-plans-are-all-over-the-map/

McKinlay, A. R., May, T., Dawes, J., Fancourt, D., & Burton, A. (2022). 'You're just there, alone in your room with your thoughts': A qualitative study about the psychosocial impact of the COVID-19 pandemic among young people living in the UK. *BMJ Open, 12*(2), e053676. http://dx.doi.org/10.1136/bmjopen-2021-053676

Miller, E. D. (2018). Cyberloneliness: The curse of the cursor? In O. Sagan & E. D. Miller (Eds.), *Narratives of loneliness: Multidisciplinary perspectives from the 21st century* (pp. 56–65). Routledge.

Mitchell, L. (2020, September 16). Opinion: The college reopening mess didn't have to happen. *CNN.* https://www.cnn.com/2020/09/16/opinions/college-reopening-financial-and-political-concerns-mitchell/index.html

Morgan, B. (2020, December 14). 3 lasting changes to grocery shopping after Covid-19. *Forbes.* https://www.forbes.com/sites/blakemorgan/2020/12/14/3-lasting-changes-to-grocery-shopping-after-covid-19/?sh=7c1765de54e7

Mulqueen, M. (2020, August 10). School reopenings are being touted as good for students' well-being, but that's wrong. *NBC News.* https://www.nbcnews.com/think/opinion/school-reopenings-are-being-touted-good-students-well-being-s-ncna1236188

Muturi, I., Freeman, S., & Banner-Lukaris, D. (2020). Virtual funerals during COVID-19 and beyond. *Innovation in Aging, 4*(Suppl 1), 966. https://doi.org/10.1093/geroni/igaa057.3530

Owens, D. (2020, August 4). Yale student sues university claiming online courses were inferior, seeks tuition refund, class action status. *Hartford Courant.* https://www.courant.com/coronavirus/hc-news-coronavirus-student-sues-yale-20200804-eyr4lbjs2nhz7lapjgvrtnyyea-story.html

Pennino, E., Ishikawa, C., Hajra, S., Singh, N., & McDonald, K. (2022). Student anxiety and engagement with online instruction across two semesters of

COVID-19 disruptions. *Journal of Microbiology & Biology Education, 23*(1), e00261-21. https://doi.org/10.1128/jmbe.00261-21

Regehr, C., & Goel, V. (2020). Managing COVID-19 in a large urban research-intensive university. *Journal of Loss and Trauma, 25*(6-7), 523-539. https://doi.org/10.1080/15325024.2020.1771846

Richards, Z. (2020, September 29). WH pressured CDC to downplay risk to children in reopening schools. *Talking Points Memo.* https://talkingpointsmemo.com/news/wh-pressured-cdc-to-downplay-risk-to-children-in-reopening-schools

Seltzer, R. (2020, August 26). Running numbers or running from numbers? *Inside Higher Ed.* https://www.insidehighered.com/news/2020/08/26/major-public-universities-havent-always-been-forthcoming-statistical-modeling-fall

Stelloh, T., & Alexander, B. (2020, August 9). Nine people test positive for coronavirus at Georgia school captured in viral images. *NBC News.* https://www.nbcnews.com/news/us-news/nine-people-test-positive-coronavirus-georgia-school-captured-viral-images-n1236249

Valeii, K. (2020, August 20). Teachers and students shouldn't be Covid-19 experiments in the fall. *CNN.* https://www.cnn.com/2020/07/30/opinions/teachers-students-school-year-covid-19-valeii/index.html

Vasel, K. (2021, March). The pandemic forced a massive remote-work experiment. Now comes the hard part. *CNN.* https://www.cnn.com/2021/03/09/success/remote-work-covid-pandemic-one-year-later/index.html

Walsh, B. (2020, December 12). The death spiral of public life. *Axios.* https://www.axios.com/coronavirus-death-spiral-schools-transit-restaurants-ac9b310b-aca1-477c-97b2-2a5193584873.html

Wasson Simpson, K. S., & Muise, M. D. (2022). "I wish there was a guide": Navigating changes to intimate relationship scripts during the COVID-19 pandemic in 2020. *The Canadian Journal of Human Sexuality, 31*(2), 268-279. https://doi.org/10.3138/cjhs.2022-0016

Wilson, M. (2020, April 2/6). What New York looked like during the 1918 flu pandemic. *The New York Times.* https://www.nytimes.com/2020/04/02/nyregion/spanish-flu-nyc-virus.html

CHAPTER TEN

Epilogue: Where Do We Go From Here?

This concluding chapter aims to synthesize and summarize select key themes from the previous chapters. In doing so, it also offers some suggestions and insights about how everyday life may continue to function in the wake and aftermath of the coronavirus pandemic.

You Can't Unscramble an Egg

Just a few months after the pandemic began, in June 2020, a Harris Poll revealed that 86% of their sample of American adults were "concerned" about how the pandemic was impacting their everyday life with 73% endorsing a belief that whenever life became "normal," they would retain many of their newly found modalities of behavior (Valentic, 2020). Some of these reported changes—such as 28% of their sample suggesting that they would wear gloves "most of the time" in public locations—would likely now seem dubious insomuch that they may have been more reflective of broader concerns pertaining to limited knowledge of the virus at the time (such as an early concern about the transmissibility of how it was believed to spread on surfaces; Barber, 2020). A problem with this notion of "normal" is that, to the degree that individuals may be expecting a life and world *exactly* as it was pre-Covid, such individuals are likely to be greatly disappointed. In July 2020, 75% of Americans feared that life would never revert back to what was once viewed as "normal" (Anderer, 2020). Indeed, we cannot go backwards in time to a world without Covid. Historically though, all pandemics have indeed ended (Collinson, 2021). Yet, the virus itself—like most viruses, including the 1918 influenza—is unlikely to disappear. The virus responsible for the world's last great pandemic never truly went away (and its genetic lineage can still be found in contemporary seasonal flus); however, the hope is, like the 1918 influenza, Covid will become less virulent and the larger population will be less likely to experience serious consequences from it (Roos, 2020).

Even though an AP-NORC survey found that Americans were between 7-25% more likely to engage in common activities like visiting friends or going to a restaurant, gym, or theatre from May 2020 to June 2021 (Sainz & Fingerhut, 2021), another survey released in June 2021 suggested that half of its American sample seriously questioned whether they would ever recover from their pandemic-related stress (Melore, 2021). As an editor for a magazine produced by the American Institute of Stress aptly put it (also) in June 2021: "It's not likely somebody put a period on the sentence, and we're done with this pandemic. We really don't know what's ahead..." (LaMotte, 2021, p. 1). As also discussed in the aforementioned article, the emotional energy and hypervigilance in trying to function with our everyday lives was not just psychologically jarring but also demanded much neurocognitive work; as such, individuals may show anything between the two seemingly different extremes of feeling exhilarated by the prospect of somehow now being able to modify their pandemic routine to feeling a sense of worry or concern about how (or even whether) to return to their pre-pandemic regimen (or at least modify it); though seeking out therapy may be appropriate in cases where an individual feels overwhelmed by such patterns, self-compassion should be cultivated.

Possible Societal and Personal Changes

Attempting to make any conclusive statements about how our personal and collective worlds might generally change may be foolish to do so especially since (at the time of this writing around two years after the virus was first detected in China) there have been many relatively unexpected shifts that the pandemic took (e.g., Hamblin, 2021). For instance, in April 2021, Kershner (2021) wrote glowingly about the promise and potential to safely and freely engage in everyday pre-pandemic behavior without cause for concern in Israel since its population was largely vaccinated—but then came the Delta variant and, importantly, more data from Israel that a vaccine booster might be prudent, particularly for vulnerable populations. And, in early November 2021, the World Health Organization's (WHO) European head, Hans Kluge, issued a media briefing of "grave concern" of European Covid spread entering into the winter 2021-2022 season (Strauss, 2021); that development is another reminder that as long as the virus continues to remain in any given area of the world, it remains a potential threat to all. Indeed, in July 2020, Zhang (2020) offered another caution that was painfully prescient such that the availability of vaccines should not at all necessarily suggest the end of the pandemic or virus. Among some of her stated concerns was the dubious (and realized) possibility that enough of the population would be appropriately vaccinated, along with the unknown preventive quality of the vaccines coupled with the unpredictability of the virus.

Tragically, just a few weeks after the aforementioned WHO warning, the world saw the dawn of a new Covid variant, Omicron, which proved to be even more contagious (but less deadly) than Delta. Around that time, in December 2021, similar pronouncements were made about the potential spread of the Omicron variant—like "The variant will not discriminate by state lines" (Cullinane, 2021)—that echoed cautions from the start of the pandemic. In fact, noted epidemiologist Dr. Michael Osterholm, to whom the aforesaid statement was attributed (and who recognized by January 20, 2020, that the world was about to face a pandemic), had previously (in August 2020) stated that he felt that Covid would likely be a disease that would remain for decades and that it was a misnomer to view it as a virus that merely came and went in waves like the 1918 influenza pandemic or that vaccines would automatically eliminate it (Lee, 2020). Even if the vaccines provided a permanent end to the virus, many will likely be suffering from the physical effects of Covid for decades to come (Guzman, 2020)—let alone the psychological scars. In the summer of 2020, there was a concern that the initial batch of Covid vaccines could be mediocre and it might take some time to perfect more effective ones (Johnson, 2020). What this (and related analyses) failed to fully consider was both the ever-changing nature of the virus itself—particularly with respect to the Delta and Omicron variants—and the effects caused by significant portions of both the American and global population refusing (or, in the case of poorer countries, lacking the ability) to vaccinate. The aforementioned article noted that: "On April 12, 1955, a vaccine against polio was shown effective and safe. Its inventor, Jonas Salk, became a national hero. Church bells rang, and people ran into the streets to hug one another..." (Johnson, 2020, p. 3). Many individuals reported feeling quite an array of emotions once they were able to get the Covid vaccine that were largely, though not exclusively, positive (Wellington, 2021). But, in the year following the Covid vaccine's release to the public, America has lacked the collective sense of joy that may have been heralded with respect to the arrival of the polio vaccine.

At the end of 2020, Yong (2020) suggested that a growing consensus amongst public health officials was that there was much potential for a more positive outlook regarding the state of the pandemic one year later with a few caveats—including, most notably, an uncertainty of how the virus itself would evolve and the vaccination rate. While that more optimistic forecast proved to be reasonably accurate, regrettably, so did the realities about the significant portion of Americans who chose not to vaccinate particularly as the Delta variant became even more transmissible than the original virus. Indeed, as all viruses continue to mutate and evolve, it is virtually impossible to predict its next course—though the hope still remains that outbreaks will continue to diminish as vaccination rates increase and therapeutic treatments continue to advance (e.g., Torjesen, 2021). Perhaps in a desire to put the pandemic behind us, it may be tempting to feel like none of the behavioral changes or experiences we may have made during the pandemic should be maintained moving forward. But, some have argued that there are a host of behaviors that should be retained and even cultivated, such as, from the relatively mundane (such as wearing masks when sick and walking and savoring the outdoors) to interpersonal (such as tending to older parents and relatives more sensitively and fostering virtual connections with loved ones when not feasible to physically visit) and intrapersonal changes (such as being more mindful of class differences and our own sense of mortality; NBC News, 2021). But more broadly, as Robertson and Doshi (2021) have put it, "the end of the pandemic will not be televised" insomuch that there are no universally agreed upon metrics to unequivocally state when a pandemic has ended.

Though Covid may never truly disappear, as Georges Benjamin, the executive director of the American Public Health Association, aptly put it: "…pandemics end because the disease is unable to transmit itself through people or other vectors that allow the transmission of the disease…" (Roy, 2021, p. 14). In that respect, perhaps a more important question to ask is what will our world look like assuming there is some collective technical agreement that the pandemic has ended and the disease has entered a more endemic stage. In his book, "Ten Lessons for a Post-Pandemic World," noted journalist Fareed Zakaria (2020) highlights human resilience in the face of great upheaval and he also offers some tangible observations about (among other points) the importance of competent leaders and the continued significance of the Internet as well as cautions about inequities. Even though he makes it clear that his analysis is not about the pandemic per se, he does add:

> Any large shock can have diverse effects, depending on the state of the world at the time and on how human beings react—with fear or denial or adaptation. In the case of the novel coronavirus, the impact is being shaped by the reality that the world is deeply interconnected, that most countries were unprepared for the pandemic, and that in its wake, many of them…shut down their societies and economies in a manner unprecedented in human history…What exactly are the consequences of the pandemic?…The post-pandemic world is going to be, in many respects, a sped-up version of the world we knew. But when you put life on fast-forward, events no longer proceed naturally, and the consequences can be disruptive, even deadly…Post-pandemic life will be different for countries, companies, and especially individuals. Even if economics and politics return to normal, human beings will not. They will have been through an unusual, difficult trial and have a sense of newfound, hard won opportunity (Zakaria, 2020, pp. 1-2).

Many scholars, though, have offered a rather gloomy, if not dire, assessment of the long-term effects of the pandemic. A report featuring several eminent psychologists (Seitz et al., 2020) has suggested that the pandemic has helped to reveal several evolutionary psychological insights featuring many individual, interpersonal, and larger societal concerns; among these key troubling trends were a decline in planned pregnancies, singles less likely to form relationships, and increased struggles for women (in particular) trying to navigate childcare and work responsibilities. Perhaps even more concerning is that, unlike in past calamities, the United States has not shown increases in compassion or kindness (perhaps in part because the pandemic has caused many Americans to want to retain their individuality and challenge authority).

To further accentuate these concerning assessments, as first noted in the preface of this book, in late February 2022, Russian President Vladimir Putin ordered a full-blown attack of its peaceful neighboring country of Ukraine in an overtly aggressive act. At the time of this writing, it is not exactly clear what the longer-term fallout will be (geopolitical or otherwise) or what exactly is Putin's gameplan save for the attempted occupation of Ukraine—which, by some American and British accounts, could last for years or decades (Weber, 2022). The concerns associated with this invasion, which is the largest since the end of World War II, by a nuclear power with a reportedly unstable leader are aplenty though—from forever altering the global order (Campbell, 2022) to the suffering and potential humanitarian crisis in Ukraine (and even surrounding bordering countries; Banco et al., 2022). There has even been some consideration of the public health concerns emanating from this crisis, including the possibility of prolonging the Covid pandemic (Lee, 2022). And, this invasion may have trigged new bouts of anxiety and depression for Americans who were just trying to rebound from two years of coping with the pandemic as the Omicron surge appeared to ebb (Carcamo et al., 2022). Perhaps if there has been any solace in this belligerent invasion it has been the tremendous bravery exhibited by the Ukrainian people and its leaders, headed by their President Volodymyr Zelensky, to thwart Russia's aggression (Rubin, 2022).

Is the Covid-19 Pandemic Really The "Loss and Trauma of Our Time?"

On May 27, 2020, acclaimed Associated Press reporter Ted Anthony wrote an article: "American virus deaths at 100,000: What does a number mean?" (Anthony, 2020). In this article, Anthony posed this question to a number of scholars. For instance, Rhodes College history professor Jeffrey Jackson stated: "We all want to measure these experiences because they're so shocking, so overwhelming that we want to bring some sense of knowability to the unknown" (p. 2). In that vein, Anthony (2020) noted the prominent work of historian Drew Gilpin Faust who has written extensively about the meaning of death in the American Civil War to which Anthony added: "Facing such massive death and challenges counting the dead, Americans started to realize that numbers and statistics represented more than knowledge; they contained power…" (p. 2). Anthony (2020) also featured this statement from psychology professor Daryl Van Tongeren: "Each day we've become accustomed to the new reality that we don't realize how far we've traveled from what normal is…With too much suffering over time, it's overwhelming and we begin to become callous. And our empathy essentially runs out… We're so accustomed to death right now, at 100,000, that our empathy has become lower" (pp. 4-5).

It is particularly telling that Anthony's (2020) analysis notes that—at that point in time, the number of U.S. Covid deaths had already surpassed the number of American deaths from 9/11 and the Korean and Vietnam Wars. At that point (in late May 2020), the U.S. had not reached the death toll of—which up to this time —had been the events associated with the most American deaths: World War I (more than 116,000), World War II (more than 405,000) and the U.S. Civil War (more than 655,000). By September 2021, the U.S. Covid-death toll had not only overtaken *all* of those events, but it also surpassed the approximate 675,000 Americans who died as a result of the 1918 influenza pandemic (Branswell, 2021) making the Covid-19 pandemic the deadliest event in American history to date (as of late 2021). Anthony (2020) correctly notes that context matters in understanding the numbers of deaths just as I expressed in my own earlier consideration (Miller, 2020) of the meaning of deaths from the pandemic. Consistent with another paper where I detailed how we find meaning in the losses from 9/11 on the tenth anniversary of those attacks (Miller, 2011), in some respects, comparing such death rates almost seems irrelevant if not downright cruel: For instance, just because the deaths from the pandemic vastly outnumber the number of deaths from the 9/11 attacks certainly should not cause us in any way to view those deaths somehow with less solace. Regarding the pandemic, one could even make the point that *on a per capita basis* (i.e., factoring in the U.S. population at the time), that the death toll was not necessarily as severe as many of the aforesaid events. Psychologists and other social scientists have long appreciated the bevy of logical fallacies that people often make in everyday life decision-making and comparisons such as the aforementioned examples (e.g., Fantino et al., 2003).

Anthony (2020) also notes how the stark number of six million Jews murdered in the Holocaust both humanizes those atrocities but also "is a figure so enormous that it resists comprehension" (p. 4). Death tolls, he further suggests, can be a means of classifying events and a strong implication of what an event signified. On that 100,000 U.S. death toll mark, he ended his critique by adding: "Just as 100,000 means something this week in American life. Maybe not everything — not a vaccine, not a treatment — and maybe not clarity, exactly. Not yet. But something" (p. 6).

So, what exactly is that "something?" Trying to compare difficult or traumatic events is generally a subjective exercise at some level. For instance, a group of 28 historians were asked if 2020 was the "worst" year in history. While these historians argued that it clearly was not—and reminded that there were several other even more perilous world and American events—such as the height of the Black Death in 1348, the Holocaust, or the U.S. Civil War (particularly in 1862, where it was not clear if America might collapse)—these same historians ranked the year of 2020 amongst the eighth worse years in American history (Rosenwald, 2020).

The theme of how we can somehow codify or categorize different gradients or levels of evil remains a challenging one (Miller, 2019). However, most people still have a commonplace understanding of how to make sense of it; for instance, while most individuals would likely agree that any act of violence is deeply troubling, if it is committed in the name of genocide, we might view it as even more so (Berkowitz, 1999). To put this in the context of the pandemic, it is very difficult to universally say that everyone has viewed it the same way—just as psychologists have long known that stress is often interpreted in very idiosyncratic and personal ways (Hobfoll, 1989). For instance, some may have taken preventative measures throughout the pandemic whereas others viewed it as a hoax. Some may have suffered personal losses due to the pandemic, while others may have just viewed it as an inconvenience.

Some might say that some of the more noxious behavior shown during the pandemic was especially jarring—from those who refused to vaccinate or wildly spread misinformation to those who carried out behaviors in the name of hate. Certainly, such odious acts are just that. And, it is questionable how a country can run effectively when a sizable portion of its citizenry and its leaders hold an indifferent—or worse, callous—view to a serious public health crisis. But, as particularly explored in Chapter 7, both history and social psychology have long shown that human destructiveness can be potentially found and realized within any of us. Stanley Milgram, the experimenter behind the legendary obedience studies, once said:

> … that if a system of death camps were set up in the United States of the sort we had seen in Nazi Germany, one would be able to find sufficient personnel for those camps in any medium-sized American town (Blass, 1999, p. 955).

We should also learn from the disparities caused or exacerbated both within and outside of America during the pandemic—even though such disparities were widely known and studied well before (World Health Organization, 2013). Likewise, even if we can never fully ascertain the precise source of the original virus, the pandemic should reinforce the crucial importance of respecting and encouraging a healthy physical environment (United Nations, 2021)—and yet, this too was a lesson we should have known.

If all of these "lessons" of the pandemic really are extensions of well-known exemplars of human behavior as demonstrated by previous models and examples from history, psychology, and social science, then a reasonable question to ask and wonder is why would I have termed the pandemic as "the loss and trauma of our time" in March/April 2020 (Miller, 2020)—and is it really that? To answer the latter part of that question first, once more, how we—individually and collectively—look at and understand the effects of the pandemic will almost certainly change over time and many of these effects will simply not fully be known or realized until some future point (as the Russian invasion of Ukraine offers one such possible example of that point).

However, in March/April 2020, the pandemic struck me—as an event—as one that was fraught with much potential stress for a prolonged period. All of us have at least been challenged during the pandemic, even if we may not necessarily view what we have experienced as a "major loss" (Harvey & Miller, 1998). In considering about how people make sense of loss experiences, Harvey (2000) wrote:

> ... people often conceive their losses in terms of accounts or stories that contextualize the major events of their lives...In people's stories involving major loss, they may assimilate different loss events occurring at quite different points in time as related and meaningful to who we have become (p. 7).

Historically, psychologists have largely found that adult personality generally tends to remain fairly stable over time (Heatherton & Weinberger, 1994). But, consistent with Harvey's (2000) previous point, all of us will likely have stories to tell about the pandemic—and many of them will feature some degree of loss. How we understand and explain these stories to ourselves and others will certainly continue to evolve over time as well. To say that everyone will think back to the pandemic and unequivocally say it was traumatic would probably not be accurate. But, to the degree that it has at least universally created that potential, it is—as an event—very unique.

In reflecting on this entire book as a whole, it is difficult to fathom how Americans (and, indeed, the world) will continue to reckon with the legacy of the Covid pandemic—but will likely do so for years to come. Of course, the Covid pandemic has provided many lessons in order to prevent (Gates, 2022) or at least prepare for the next pandemic (Sridhar, 2022). But, even if individuals have generally coped well during and after the immediate initial shock of the pandemic's reality and occurrence, it still may have personally impacted us in ways that may not be necessarily clear for years to come as we continue to make sense of it. More broadly, as a society, we will have to somehow come to terms with the troublesome or disturbing behaviors displayed during the pandemic as well. Academics and laypersons alike will certainly continue to revisit and revise these interpretations and potentially ever-changing effects for generations to come.

References

Anderer, J. (2020, July 21). Nostalgic for 2019: Three in four Americans worry life will never go back to 'normal'. *Study Finds.* https://www.studyfinds.org/nostalgic-for-2019-americans-worry-life-will-never-go-back-to-normal/

Anthony, T. (2020, May 27). American virus deaths at 100,000: What does a number mean? *AP News.* https://apnews.com/f768f47203908b834e245fbf7f0b3ccc

Banco, E., Swan, B. W., & Bencharif, S. T. (2022, February 28). U. S. officials: Russian escalation in Ukraine could lead to humanitarian crisis. *Politico.* https://www.politico.com/news/2022/02/28/u-s-officials-russian-escalation-in-ukraine-could-lead-to-humanitarian-crisis-00012548

Barber, G. (2020, October 20). It's time to talk about Covid-19 and surfaces again. *Wired.* https://www.wired.com/story/its-time-to-talk-about-covid-19-and-surfaces-again

Berkowitz, L. (1999). Evil is more than banal: Situationism and the concept of evil. *Personality and Social Psychology Review, 3*(3), 246-253. https://doi.org/10.1207/s15327957pspr0303_7

Blass, T. (1999). The Milgram paradigm after 35 years: Some things we now know about obedience to authority. *Journal of Applied Social Psychology, 29*(5), 955-978. https://doi.org/10.1111/j.1559-1816.1999.tb00134.x

Branswell, H. (2021, September 20). Covid-19 overtakes 1918 Spanish flu as deadliest disease in American history. *STAT.* https://www.statnews.com/2021/09/20/covid-19-set-to-overtake-1918-spanish-flu-as-deadliest-disease-in-american-history/

Campbell, C. (2022, February 24). How Russia's invasion of Ukraine could change the global order forever. *Time.* https://time.com/6150874/world-order-russia-ukraine/

Carcamo, C., Reyes-Velarde, A., & Nelson, L. J. (2022, February 24). First pandemic. Then recession. Now, Russia invades Ukraine. Anything else, world? *Los Angeles Times.* https://www.latimes.com/california/story/2022-02-24/pandemic-recession-russia-ukraine-war-anxiety-mental-health

Collinson, S. (2021, May 25). A vaccine marvel is bringing America back. *CNN.* https://www.cnn.com/2021/05/25/politics/vaccine-marvel-america-back/index.html

Cullinane, S. (2021, December 22). Omicron will not recognize state lines when it storms the US, expert says. *CNN.* https://www.cnn.com/2021/12/21/health/us-coronavirus-tuesday/index.html

Fantino, E., Stolarz-Fantino, S., & Navarro, A. (2003). Logical fallacies: A behavioral approach to reasoning. *The Behavior Analyst Today, 4*(1), 109–117. https://doi.org/10.1037/h0100014

Gates, B. (2022). *How to prevent the next pandemic.* Alfred A. Knopf.

Guzman, J. (2020, July 31). The effects of the coronavirus pandemic will be 'felt for decades to come,' WHO chief says. *The Hill.* https://thehill.com/changing-america/resilience/natural-disasters/510001-the-effects-of-the-coronavirus-pandemic-will-be

Hamblin, J. (2021, March 26). COVID-19 is different now. *The Atlantic.* https://
www.theatlantic.com/health/archive/2021/03/covid-19-variants-covid-21/
618427/

Harvey, J. H. (2000). *Give sorrow words: Perspectives on loss and trauma.* Taylor
& Francis.

Harvey, J. H., & Miller, E. D. (1998). Toward a psychology of loss. *Psychological
Science, 9*(6), 429-434. https://doi.org/10.1111/1467-9280.00081

Heatherton, T. F., & Weinberger, J. L. (Eds.). (1994). *Can personality change?*
American Psychological Association. https://doi.org/10.1037/10143-000

Hobfoll, S. E. (1989). Conservation of resources: A new attempt at conceptualizing
stress. *American Psychologist, 44*(3), 513-524. https://doi.org/10.1037/0003-
066X.44.3.513

Johnson, C. Y. (2020, August 2). A coronavirus vaccine won't change the world
right away. *The Washington Post.* https://www.washingtonpost.com/health/
2020/08/02/covid-vaccine/

Kershner, I. (2021, April 5/May 17). My life in Israel's brave new post-pandemic
future. *The New York Times.* https://www.nytimes.com/2021/04/05/world/
middleeast/israel-vaccinations.html

LaMotte, S. (2021, June 30). Anxious as we transition out of the pandemic? That's
common and can be treated, experts say. *CNN.* https://www.cnn.com/2021/
06/30/health/anxiety-pandemic-opening-wellness/index.html

Lee, B. Y. (2022, Russia's invasion of Ukraine may cause polio, Covid-19, public
health crises. *Forbes.* https://www.forbes.com/sites/brucelee/2022/02/26/
russias-invasion-of-ukraine-may-cause-polio-covid-19-public-health-crises

Lee, J. (2020, August 1). Dr. Osterholm: Americans will be living with the coronavirus
for decades. *MarketWatch.* https://www.marketwatch.com/story/osterholm
-americans-will-be-living-with-the-coronavirus-for-decades-2020-07-30

Melore, C. (2021, June 18). Half of Americans fear they'll never fully recover
from COVID pandemic stress. *Study Finds.* https://www.studyfinds.org/half-
americans-will-never-recover-pandemic-stress/

Miller, E. D. (2011). Finding meaning at Ground Zero for future generations:
Some reflections a decade after 9/11. *International Social Science Review,
86*(3/4), 113-133. https://www.jstor.org/stable/41887494

Miller, E. D. (2019). Codifying gradients of evil in select YouTube comment
postings. *Human Behavior and Emerging Technologies, 1*(3), 216-222. https://
doi.org/10.1002/hbe2.155

Miller, E. D. (2020). The COVID-19 pandemic: The loss and trauma event of our
time. *Journal of Loss and Trauma, 25*(6-7), 560-572. https://doi.org/10.1080/
15325024.2020.175921

NBC News. (2021, April 9). What we should keep post-pandemic. *NBC News.*
https://www.nbcnews.com/specials/what-we-should-keep-post-pandemic/
index.html

Robertson, D., & Doshi, P. (2021). The end of the pandemic will not be televised.
BMJ, 375, e068094. https://doi.org/10.1136/bmj-2021-068094

Roos, D. (2020, December 11). Why the 1918 flu pandemic never really ended.
History. https://www.history.com/news/1918-flu-pandemic-never-ended

Rosenwald, M. S. (2020, December 30). Was 2020 the worst year ever? Historians weigh in. *The Washington Post*. https://www.washingtonpost.com/history/2020/12/30/ranking-2020-worst-year-history/

Roy, J. (2021, December 23). Will this pandemic ever end? Here's what happened with the last ones. *Los Angeles Times*. https://www.latimes.com/science/story/2021-12-23/will-the-pandemic-ever-end-heres-what-happened-with-the-last-ones

Rubin, J. (2022, February 27). Opinion: Distinguished persons of the week: Breathtaking bravery in the face of war. *The Washington Post*. https://www.washingtonpost.com/opinions/2022/02/27/distinguished-persons-ukraine/

Sainz, A., & Fingerhut, H. (2021, June 18). AP-NORC poll: Many Americans resuming pre-virus activities. *AP News*. https://apnews.com/article/only-on-ap-lifestyle-coronavirus-pandemic-health-ddfd165dd67e9ec79d4850a1d80734e8

Seitz, B. M., Aktipis, A., Buss, D. M., Alcock, J., Bloom, P., Gelfand, M. J Harris, S., Lieberman, D., Horowitz, B. N., Pinker, S., Wilson, D., & Haselton, M. G. (2020). The pandemic exposes human nature: 10 evolutionary insights. *Proceedings of the National Academy of Sciences, 117*(45), 27767-27776. https://doi.org/10.1073/pnas.2009787117

Sridhar, D. (2022). Five ways to prepare for the next pandemic. *Nature, 610*, S50. https://doi.org/10.1038/d41586-022-03362-8

Strauss, M. (2021, November 4). Covid rates in Europe are of 'grave concern', warns WHO. *Independent*. https://www.independent.co.uk/news/world/europe/covid-cases-coronavirus-europe-who-b1951538.html

Torjesen, I. (2021). Covid-19 will become endemic but with decreased potency over time, scientists believe. *BMJ: British Medical Journal (Online), 372*. https://doi.org/ 10.1136/bmj.n494

United Nations. (2021, October 15). The human right to a clean and healthy environment: 6 things you need to know. *UN News*. https://news.un.org/en/story/2021/10/1103082

Valentic, S. (2020, June 4). Most Americans expect life to never return to normal. *EHS Today*. https://www.ehstoday.com/covid19/article/21133121/study-most-americans-expect-life-to-never-return-to-normal

Weber, P. (2022, March 2). U. S. and Britain reportedly believe the Ukraine war could last 10-20 years, become a Russian quagmire. *The Week*. https://theweek.com/russo-ukrainian-war/1010797/us-and-britain-reportedly-believe-the-ukraine-war-could-last-10-20

Wellington, (2021, April 15). It's normal to feel emotional about the vaccine. Here's why it's a roller coaster. *The Philadelphia Inquirer*. https://www.inquirer.com/philly-tips/covid-vaccine-emotions-20210415.html

World Health Organization. (2013). *The economics of the social determinants of health and health inequalities: A resource book*. World Health Organization.

Yong, E. (2020, December 29). Where year two of the pandemic will take us. *The Atlantic*. https://www.theatlantic.com/health/archive/2020/12/pandemic-year-two/617528/

Zakaria, F. (2020). *Ten lessons for a post-pandemic world*. W. W. Norton & Company.

Zhang, S. (2020, July 24/25). A vaccine reality check. *The Atlantic*. https://www.theatlantic.com/health/archive/2020/07/covid-19-vaccine-reality-check/614566/

Index

A

accounts. *see* stories (personal)
American Psychological
   Association, 39, 51, 100
anti-Asian, 61, 79, 80
anti-Semitism, 29, 79
anti-science, 7, 29, 77
anxiety, 39, 42, 43, 44, 45, 51-52,
   60, 76, 100, 102, 113
authoritarianism, 13, 80. *see also*
   nationalism; societal concerns
   and threats (overview)

B

Biden, Joseph (and Administration
   of), 2, 14, 19-20, 29, 31, 41, 93
Birx, Deborah, 17, 19, 74

C

caregiving, 42, 59, 64-65
Centers for Disease Control and
   Prevention (CDC), 1, 19, 20, 28,
   51, 52, 59, 63, 103
China, 2, 8, 14-15, 17, 79, 110
Class of 2020, 44, 88. *see also*
   young adults
close relationship challenges
   (overview), 42-44. *see also*
   caregiving; domestic violence;
   divorce; friendships; Internet-
   related behaviors
cognitive dissonance, 77, 88
cognitive heuristics, 92, 114
college experiences, 43-44, 103-
   104. *see also* online schooling

compromised health conditions
   (related to pandemic), 44, 54,
   59-60, 61, 64, 65, 92, 102
conspiracy theories, 31, 78, 79
coping, xii, 39, 42, 51, 52, 53, 54,
   55, 60, 102, 110, 111-112, 113,
   116

D

death tolls, 61, 74-75, 89, 113-114
deindividuation, 80
democracy and democratic
   liberties, 30, 31, 32, 75, 77, 79
Democratic public opinion,
   Republican public opinion *vs.*,
   5, 7, 32, 75, 93, 103
Democratic responses (political)
   to the pandemic, 15-16, 17, 18,
   28, 89-90. *see also* Biden,
   Joseph (and Administration of)
denial, 7, 18-19, 77, 78, 80, 112
depression (psychological), 41, 45,
   51, 52, 60, 100, 102, 113
divorce, 42, 53
domestic violence, 39, 43

E

E-commerce. *see* stay at home
   economy
economic changes, 4, 14, 15, 16,
   18, 19, 27-28, 30-34, 39, 43, 61,
   63, 65, 89, 99, 101, 104, 112. *see
   also* societal concerns and
   threats (overview); stay at
   home economy
elderly adults, 16, 43, 55, 59-60, 64,
   65, 92, 111

elections, 15, 19, 32, 93
environmental and architectural
    concerns, 4, 55, 91, 93, 115
evil (as a concept), 9, 64, 73, 115
experiments and experimental
    descriptions of the pandemic,
    2-4

F

Fauci, Anthony, ix, 15, 17, 18-19,
    28, 77
Floyd, George (murder of and
    subsequent protests), 4, 30, 62-
    64, 67
freedom (sense of). *see*
    individualism and
    individualistic
friendships, 15, 40, 44-45, 99-100,
    109. *see also* close relationship
    challenges (overview)
funerals, 40, 53, 54, 100. *see also*
    grief; loss

G

Garrett, Laurie, 13
Gates, Bill, 13, 78, 116
gender differences, 3, 44, 45, 51,
    64, 65, 76, 100, 101, 102, 112. *see
    also* caregiving
Generation Z. *see* Class of 2020;
    young adults
Great Resignation, 27
grief, 21, 39, 51, 52, 53-56. *see also*
    loss

H

health belief model, 76
health disparities, 61, 92, 115

healthcare professionals (as
    heroes), 73-74
helping behavior, 20, 73-74
historian assessments of the
    pandemic, 113-115
HIV/AIDS, 18, 30, 53, 77, 80, 89
Holocaust, 9, 20, 79, 114, 115. *see
    also* anti-Semitism
homeless, 15, 59, 66
homophobia, 79, 80

I

immunocompromised. *see*
    compromised health
    conditions (related to
    pandemic)
impatience (regarding pandemic
    length), x, 40-41
indifference (to pandemic), 74-77,
    81, 115
individualism and individualistic,
    5, 6, 7, 13, 20, 40, 75, 76, 77, 113
influenza pandemic of 1918, 16,
    17, 19, 30, 89, 99, 109, 111, 114
Internet-related behaviors, 8, 9,
    29, 31, 32, 41, 44, 53, 54, 61, 63,
    65, 77, 78, 79, 80, 90, 92, 99-100,
    102, 103, 112. *see also* online
    schooling; stay at home
    economy; telecommuting;
    Twitter/Tweets; YouTube;
    Zoombombing

J

January 6, 2021 U.S. Capitol
    attacks, 4, 31-32, 78, 80. *see also*
    societal concerns and threats
    (overview)

L

languishing, 52-53
lockdowns. *see* shutdowns
loneliness, 31, 39, 43, 44-45, 55, 60
81, 100
long COVID, 59, 111. *see also*
compromised health
conditions (related to
pandemic)
loss, ix, xi, 2, 3, 18, 27, 40, 42, 44,
51, 53-56, 60, 88, 89, 102, 113-
116. *see also* grief

M

mandates (governmental), 13, 16,
28-30, 31, 51, 74, 76, 77, 78, 79,
99
mask wearing, 1, 5-7, 15, 16, 17,
18, 20, 28, 29, 30, 40, 41, 44, 45,
54, 74, 75, 76, 77, 78, 80, 93, 99,
102, 111
misinformation, 19, 31, 62, 78, 79,
115
murder rates, 31

N

nationalism, 32, 78, 79. *see also*
authoritarianism; societal
concerns and threats
(overview)
New York (City and State), 4, 5-8,
15-16, 66, 77, 87, 88, 89-91

O

office work, 27, 91, 100-101, 105.
see also telecommuting
online schooling, 44, 52, 88, 99,
100, 101-105

origins of coronavirus, 14-15, 18,
115. *see also* China

P

personal protective equipment
(PPE), 73, 78. *see also* mask
wearing
personality and individual
difference variables, 39, 44, 45,
56, 60, 61, 76, 88, 100, 102, 116
"plandemic", 78, 79
polarization (group and political),
31, 40, 75
post-pandemic (expectancies and
predictions), 33, 42, 80-81, 91-
92, 101, 110-113
prejudice and related hatred
(general), 31, 34, 78. *see also*
anti-Asian; anti-Semitism;
Floyd, George (murder of and
subsequent protests);
homophobia; structural
racism; sexism; transphobia
psychological reactions to
pandemic. *see* anxiety;
depression; grief; languishing;
loneliness; loss; stress
reactions; trauma
public health officials, 16, 17, 18,
19, 29, 63, 78, 111

Q

QAnon, 78. *see also* conspiracy
theories

R

racism. *see* health disparities;
prejudice and related hatred
(general); structural racism

remote learning. *see* online
schooling
Republican responses (political)
to the pandemic, 16, 28, 30, 63,
93. *see also* Trump, Donald
(and Administration of)
rural areas, 90, 92-93
Russian-Ukrainian War, ix, 4, 64,
113, 116

S

school board officials, 29-30, 78,
103
self-care. *see* coping; therapy
September 11, 2001 terrorist
attacks, 4, 5-7, 53-54, 89, 114.
see also New York (City and
State)
sexism, 29, 79
shutdowns, 3, 17, 18, 27-28, 42, 43,
45, 52, 53, 61, 63, 87-88, 90, 99,
104, 112. *see also* mandates
(governmental)
social distancing, 6, 7, 16, 18, 28,
29, 39, 41, 45, 61, 63, 74, 93, 102.
see also staying home
(psychological effects)
societal concerns and threats
(overview), 30-34. *see also*
authoritarianism; post-
pandemic (expectancies and
predictions)
socioeconomic status, 4, 14, 51,
61, 111
stay at home economy, 32-33, 87,
99
staying home (psychological
effects), xi, 5, 41, 42, 63, 74, 76,
87, 99. *see also* social distancing
stories (personal), 3, 51, 56, 116

stress reactions, 31, 32, 39, 41, 42,
43, 51, 52, 54, 55, 60, 61, 63, 64,
81, 101, 102, 109, 115, 116
structural racism, 62, 63
supply chains, 18, 30, 73

T

telecommuting, 32, 53, 61, 65, 90,
92, 99, 100. *see also* office work
terror management theory, 80
thematic analysis, 5-8
therapy, 53, 54, 110, 111. *see also*
coping
transphobia, 29
transportation and travel, xi, 14,
17, 31, 62, 88, 89, 90
trauma, ix, 1, 8, 51, 54, 55, 60, 61,
62, 113-116
Trump, Donald (and
Administration of), 6, 7, 13, 16-
19, 20, 28, 31, 40, 63, 74, 78, 79,
93, 103
Twitter/Tweets, 17-18, 53, 63, 64,
76, 77

U

urban areas, 61, 87, 88-92. *see also*
New York (City and State)

V

vaccines and vaccinations, 1, 2,
14, 15, 16, 19, 20, 28, 29, 30, 41,
45, 62, 74-79, 88, 90-93, 100-
101, 103-104, 110-111, 114-115
variants (of coronavirus), x, 2, 8,
14, 20, 28, 41, 75, 93, 104, 110,
111, 113

W

White, Ryan, 30. *see also* HIV/AIDS
World Health Organization
(WHO), 13, 14, 40, 110, 115

Y

young adults, 39, 40, 43, 45, 51, 59,
60, 100. *see also* Class of 2020;
college experiences
YouTube, 5-8, 79

Z

Zoombombing, 79. *see also*
prejudice and related hatred
(general)